A2 Chemistry
UNIT 4

AQA

Module 4: Further Physical and Organic Chemistry

Neil Goldie

Philip Allan Updates
Market Place
Deddington
Oxfordshire
OX15 0SE

tel: 01869 338652
fax: 01869 337590
e-mail: sales@philipallan.co.uk
www.philipallan.co.uk

This Guide has been written specifically to support students preparing for the AQA A2 Chemistry Unit 4 examination. The content has been neither approved nor endorsed by AQA and remains the sole responsibility of the author.

Printed by Raithby, Lawrence & Co. Ltd, Leicester

Environmental information
The paper on which this title is printed is sourced from managed, sustainable forests.

P00261

Contents

Introduction

■ ■ ■

Content Guidance

■ ■ ■

Questions and Answers

Introduction

About this guide

This guide is for students following the AQA Chemistry A2 specification. It deals with Unit 4, which examines the content of **Module 4: Further Physical and Organic Chemistry**. This unit covers 30% of the total A2 marks, or 15% of the total A-level marks. The exam consists of several structured questions, of varying length, which are all compulsory. Some questions require short answers while some are more extended, needing answers written in continuous prose. There are 90 marks available on this paper.

The key to success

It is essential that you can recall the basic facts and definitions, but a deeper understanding of the subject is necessary if you want to achieve the top grades. The key to success in chemistry is *to understand the fundamental concepts* and *be able to apply them to new and unfamiliar situations*. Good examination technique is also an important factor, enabling you to work more effectively in the exam and gain access to the marks needed for a top grade.

This guide allows you to look again at the content of the specification, test yourself at the end of each section and assess your own work. It is essential that you read through the examiner's comments because this will help you to improve your exam technique. Once you have worked through this guide, you will be aware of your weak areas and it is these that you need to address. Make a list of these problem areas and discuss them with other students in your class and with your teacher.

Using the guide

This guide has three sections:
- **Introduction** — this provides guidance on study and revision, together with advice on approaches and techniques to ensure you answer the examination questions in the best way you can.
- **Content Guidance** — this section is not intended to be a textbook. It offers guidelines on the main features of the content of Unit 4, together with particular advice on making study more productive.
- **Questions and Answers** — this shows you the sorts of questions you can expect in the unit test. Grade-A answers are provided; these are followed by examiner's comments. Careful consideration of these will improve your answers and, more importantly, will improve your understanding of the chemistry involved.

Revise a topic using the Content Guidance section as a guide. If there is something you do not understand, you should also refer to your own class notes and textbooks.

It is essential that you write down *specific* questions and discuss them with your teacher. For instance, 'Please could you explain equilibrium again' will not lead to good use of your time if you understand most of the features of equilibrium, particularly Le Chatelier's principle. 'Please could you explain K_p and calculations involving K_p, particularly partial pressures and mole fractions' is more specific and shows that you have worked hard to identify weak areas.

Once you have revised a particular topic thoroughly, you should attempt the relevant question in the Question and Answer section, *without* looking at the grade-A answer.

Compare your answer with the grade-A answer and estimate your own performance. As a rough guide, 80% = grade A, 70% = grade B, 60% = grade C etc. However, these grade boundaries are adjusted, depending on the performance of the candidates.

Read through the examiner's comments to see if you have made any of the common mistakes and to see how you could improve your technique. The comments also give some alternative answers.

Make a note of *specific questions* that caused you problems and discuss them with other students or with your teacher.

Revision schedule

- Plan your revision schedule carefully.
- It is essential that you revise regularly.
- Leave yourself enough time to cover all the material. You need to go through each topic once as a basic minimum and then go through the weak areas again.
- In the weeks leading up to the exam, it is the weak areas that you should be revising, not every topic.
- Do not try to achieve too much in each revision session. Revise one topic per session, e.g. acids and bases. Here is one way to structure your session:
  - revise from the Content Guidance section (and your own notes)
  - make a brief written summary (no more than an A4 sheet of paper)
  - attempt the question
  - mark your answer
  - read the examiner's comments
- If there are weak areas and questions that you clearly do not understand, then write down specific questions ready for discussion with your teacher.
- Finally, make sure that you attempt some past paper questions from the exam board and study the mark schemes carefully. Questions may be repeated or similar questions set.

Unit Test 4

If you have revised thoroughly, completed all the questions in this guide and discussed problems with other students and your teacher, you should enjoy the exam. If you have completed some AQA past papers, then the style of the paper will be familiar and you will recognise some questions in the exam because they will be similar to previous questions.

Do not begin to write as soon as you open the paper — quickly scan the questions first.

It is *not* essential that you answer the questions in order. If the first question is difficult, then leave it to the end. It *is* essential that you answer *all* the questions.

You will have enough time to answer all the questions, provided that you keep your answers concise and do not include irrelevant information. It is easy to waste time writing out a section of your notes that is irrelevant to the question asked. Do not repeat the question when starting your answer. The key to exam success is achieving the maximum number of marks in the minimum number of words.

The mark allocation at the end of each question should be used to estimate the amount of detail needed in your answer. If there is 1 mark available, the examiner is looking for a key word or phrase and certainly no more than one sentence. If there are 4 marks available, then you should include four key points, which usually means writing four short sentences.

No extra marks are available for producing neat answers, but it certainly helps th examiners when they are marking your work. Untidy diagrams may become inaccurate and this definitely loses marks.

Content
Guidance

This section covers the content of **Module 4: Further Physical and Organic Chemistry**. The content of this module falls into 11 sections:

- Kinetics
- Equilibria
- Acids and bases
- Nomenclature and isomerism in organic chemistry
- Compounds containing the carbonyl group
- Aromatic chemistry
- Amines
- Amino acids
- Polymers
- Organic synthesis and analysis
- Structure determination

In this Content Guidance section, the specification has been converted into user-friendly language and is in a format that is easy to remember. All the key facts, definitions and basic principles are covered. In order to achieve a top grade, it is essential that you understand fully the basic concepts and that you can apply them to unfamiliar situations.

Kinetics

This topic was covered in AS Module 2, which concentrated on the factors that are essential for a successful reaction — collision, activation energy and orientation. Module 2 also looked at the *qualitative* effect on reaction rate of changing conditions (concentration, temperature and the addition of a catalyst). All this knowledge is assumed here.

The kinetics section in Module 4 is more concerned with the *quantitative* relationship between the rate of the reaction and the concentration of the reactants, which is shown by the rate equation. You need to understand and be able to use the rate equation and be able to derive rate equations given data on initial rates and the concentrations of different reactants. You should be able to explain the qualitative effect of temperature changes on the rate constant.

Simple rate equations

The rate equation shows the relationship between the rate of reaction and the concentration of each reactant.

A typical rate equation could be:

$r = k[A]^m[B]^n$

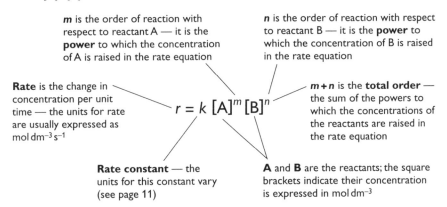

m is the order of reaction with respect to reactant A — it is the **power** to which the concentration of A is raised in the rate equation

n is the order of reaction with respect to reactant B — it is the **power** to which the concentration of B is raised in the rate equation

Rate is the change in concentration per unit time — the units for rate are usually expressed as $mol\,dm^{-3}\,s^{-1}$

$r = k\,[A]^m\,[B]^n$

m+n is the **total order** — the sum of the powers to which the concentrations of the reactants are raised in the rate equation

Rate constant — the units for this constant vary (see page 11)

A and **B** are the reactants; the square brackets indicate their concentration is expressed in $mol\,dm^{-3}$

Deriving a rate equation

The effect of concentration of a reactant on the initial rate of reaction can only be derived by experiment, it cannot be determined from the stoichiometry of the equation. Consider the following example:

A + 2B $\longrightarrow$ C + D

reactants   products

The initial rate of reaction was measured at constant temperature. The concentrations of A and B were varied and the following results obtained.

Experiment	Initial concentration of A/mol dm^{-3}	Initial concentration of B/mol dm^{-3}	Initial rate of reaction/ mol dm^{-3} s^{-1}
1	1.0	1.0	2×10^{-4}
2	2.0	1.0	8×10^{-4}
3	1.0	2.0	4×10^{-4}
4	2.0	2.0	Unknown

In experiments 1 and 2, the concentration of reactant A is doubled and the concentration of B is constant. The rate of the reaction increases by a factor of 4 (from 2×10^{-4} mol dm^{-3} s^{-1} to 8×10^{-4} mol dm^{-3} s^{-1}). The rate is proportional to $[A]^2$ and the **order is 2** with respect to reactant A.

In experiments 1 and 3, the concentration of reactant B is doubled and the concentration of A is constant. The rate of the reaction increases by a factor of 2 (from 2×10^{-4} mol dm^{-3} s^{-1} to 4×10^{-4} mol dm^{-3} s^{-1}). The rate is proportional to $[B]^1$ and the **order is 1** with respect to reactant B.

The **total order** of the reaction is $2 + 1 = 3$. This means that the rate is proportional to [concentration]^3. When comparing experiments 1 and 4, the concentration of both reactants has doubled, so the rate would be expected to go up by a factor of 2^3, i.e. 8, so the unknown rate will be 16×10^{-4} or 1.6×10^{-3} mol dm^{-3} s^{-1}.

The rate equation for this reaction is:
$r = k[A]^2[B]^1$

Calculating the rate constant, k

Rearranging the rate equation gives:

$$k = \frac{r}{[A]^2[B]^1}$$

The rate constant can then be calculated by taking the data from any experiment. For example, you can use the data from experiment 1 and then check your answer using the data from experiment 2.

- In experiment 1,

$$k = \frac{2 \times 10^{-4}}{1.0^2 \times 1.0} = 2 \times 10^{-4} \, \text{mol}^{-2} \, \text{dm}^6 \, \text{s}^{-1}$$

- In experiment 2,

$$k = \frac{8 \times 10^{-4}}{2.0^2 \times 1.0} = 2 \times 10^{-4} \, \text{mol}^{-2} \, \text{dm}^6 \, \text{s}^{-1}$$

In experiment 4, the rate constant can be used to predict the unknown rate of reaction.
$r = k[A]^2[B]^1 = 2 \times 10^{-4} \times 2.0^2 \times 2.0 = 2 \times 10^{-4} \times 8 = 1.6 \times 10^{-3}$ mol dm^{-3} s^{-1}

Units of the rate constant, k

The units of the rate constant vary according to the rate equation. Here a reaction of order 3 is used to show how to work out the units of k.

- A typical rate equation is $r = k[A]^2[B]$

- This can be rearranged as: $k = \dfrac{r}{[A]^2[B]}$

- Write out the units and cancel where possible: $\dfrac{\cancel{\text{mol dm}^{-3}}\,\text{s}^{-1}}{\cancel{\text{mol dm}^{-3}}\,\text{mol dm}^{-3}\,\text{mol dm}^{-3}}$

- Units of k: $\text{mol}^{-2}\,\text{dm}^6\,\text{s}^{-1}$

Remember:
- the units for rate are usually $\text{mol dm}^{-3}\,\text{s}^{-1}$
- the units for concentration are mol dm^{-3}
- multiplying $\text{mol} \times \text{mol} = \text{mol}^2$
- when transferring mol^2 from the bottom line to the top line it becomes mol^{-2}
- multiplying $\text{dm}^{-3} \times \text{dm}^{-3} = \text{dm}^{-6}$
- transferring dm^{-6} from the bottom line to the top line becomes dm^6

The effect of temperature on the rate constant, k

An increase in temperature always leads to an increase in the rate of the reaction. An increase in temperature causes an increase in the average kinetic energy of the particles, so they move faster and this leads to an increased collision frequency. However, a more important factor is that the increased energy means more particles now exceed the energy of activation (the minimum energy for a reaction to occur), so there are many more successful collisions. This leads to a dramatic increase in the rate of the reaction.

This can be shown on the Maxwell–Boltzmann distribution of molecular energies, where T_2 is a higher temperature than T_1.

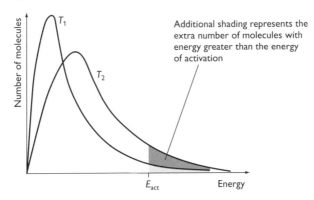

In the rate equation, $r = k[A]^m[B]^n$, the only temperature-dependent feature is the rate constant. The rate constant increases exponentially with an increase in temperature.

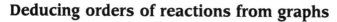

Deducing orders of reactions from graphs

These graphs will be produced from experiments that you may carry out. It is important to remember the labels on the axes and the basic shapes of the graphs.

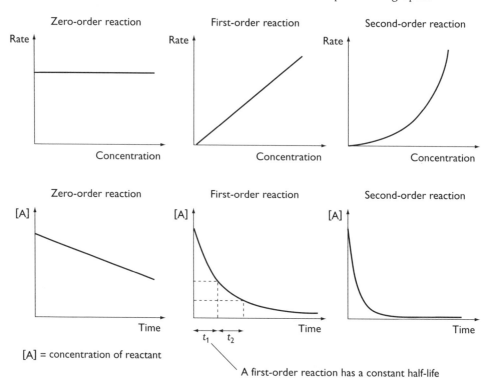

[A] = concentration of reactant

A first-order reaction has a constant half-life

Example: a typical question on kinetics

Your understanding of this topic can be checked by looking at a typical kinetics question.

The following table shows the complete results of four experiments to investigate the rate of reaction between species P, Q and R. All four experiments were carried out at the same temperature. The results for experiment 5 are incomplete.

Experiment	Initial concentration of P/mol dm^{-3}	Initial concentration of Q/mol dm^{-3}	Initial concentration of R/mol dm^{-3}	Initial rate of reaction/ mol dm^{-3} s^{-1}
1	0.01	0.01	0.02	3×10^{-5}
2	0.02	0.01	0.02	3×10^{-5}
3	0.04	0.03	0.02	9×10^{-5}
4	0.01	0.03	0.04	3.6×10^{-4}
5	0.015	0.04	0.05	Unknown

(a) Use the data to deduce the orders of the reaction with respect to P, Q and R.
(b) State the rate equation for this reaction.
(c) Calculate a value for the rate constant and deduce its units.
(d) Use the rate constant to deduce the initial rate in experiment 5.

Answers

(a) • Look at experiments 1 and 2. Doubling [P] while keeping [Q] and [R] constant has no effect on the initial rate. The order is zero with respect to P.
  • Look at experiments 1 and 3. Quadrupling [P] has no effect on the rate because the reaction is zero order with respect to P. Keeping [R] constant and tripling [Q] leads to a tripling of the initial rate. The rate is directly proportional to [Q], so it is first order with respect to Q.
  • Look at Experiments 3 and 4. Decreasing [P] has no effect on the rate because the reaction is zero order with respect to P. Keeping [Q] constant and doubling [R] leads to a quadrupling of the initial rate. The rate is proportional to $[R]^2$, so it is second order with respect to R.

(b) The rate equation is $r = k[Q][R]^2$. (Notice that [P] does not appear in the rate equation because the concentration of P has no effect on the rate.)

(c) Rearranging the rate equation, and using the data from experiment 1, gives:

$$k = \frac{r}{[Q][R]^2} = \frac{3 \times 10^{-5}}{0.01 \times 0.02^2} = 7.5 \text{ mol}^{-2}\,\text{dm}^6\,\text{s}^{-1}$$

(d) $r = k[Q][R]^2 = 7.5 \times 0.04 \times 0.05^2 = 7.5 \times 10^{-4} \text{ mol dm}^{-3}\,\text{s}^{-1}$

Equilibria

You will not be expected to define Le Chatelier's principle, but you must be able to apply it to any equilibrium reaction so that you can predict the effect on the yield of changing the concentration, the temperature and the pressure. You need to remember that only temperature affects the value of the equilibrium constants K_c and K_p. You must be able to explain why a catalyst does not affect the position of the equilibrium or the equilibrium constant.

You should be able to write expressions for K_c and K_p for equilibrium reactions and then carry out calculations involving such expressions. You need to be able to derive partial pressures from mole fractions and total pressure.

Introduction

A dynamic equilibrium is achieved when:
  • a reversible reaction takes place in a *closed system*
  • the rate of the forward reaction is *equal* to the rate of the backward reaction

- the concentrations of the reactants and products remain *constant*
- the reaction is *continuous* and is still proceeding

Equilibrium constant, K_c, for homogeneous systems

Consider the following equilibrium:

$aA + bB \rightleftharpoons cC + dD$

The equilibrium constant K_c is defined by the expression:

$$K_c = \frac{[C]^c[D]^d}{[A]^a[B]^b}$$

- 'Homogeneous' means all the species are in the same phase.
- The equilibrium concentrations of reactants and products are indicated by the value of K_c. The larger the value of K_c the more products will be present.
- The equilibrium constant K_c is calculated from molar concentrations at constant temperature. Concentrations are expressed in units of $mol\,dm^{-3}$.
- The units of K_c vary according to the number of reactants and products.
- If the numbers of moles of reactants and products are the same, then K_c will have no units.
- The value of K_c (and K_p — see later) is only dependent on temperature. A change in concentration or a change in pressure will alter the equilibrium position, but not the value of the equilibrium constant. A catalyst has *no effect* on the equilibrium position or the equilibrium constant.
- In an endothermic reaction, an increase in temperature will cause an increase in the value of K_c.
- In an exothermic reaction, an increase in temperature will cause a decrease in the value of K_c.

Examples

The table below contains the expressions for K_c for some common equilibrium reactions.

Reaction	K_c	Units
$PCl_5 \rightleftharpoons PCl_3 + Cl_2$	$K_c = \dfrac{[PCl_3][Cl_2]}{[PCl_5]}$	$mol\,dm^{-3}$
$H_2 + I_2 \rightleftharpoons 2HI$	$K_c = \dfrac{[HI]^2}{[H_2][I_2]}$	No units
$N_2 + 3H_2 \rightleftharpoons 2NH_3$	$K_c = \dfrac{[NH_3]^2}{[N_2][H_2]^3}$	$mol^{-2}\,dm^6$
$2SO_2 + O_2 \rightleftharpoons 2SO_3$	$K_c = \dfrac{[SO_3]^2}{[SO_2]^2[O_2]}$	$mol^{-1}\,dm^3$

Calculations involving K_c

Example: the decomposition of phosphorus(V) chloride

1.33 mol of phosphorus(V) chloride vapour was heated to 500 K in a vessel of volume 15 dm³. The equilibrium mixture contained 0.8 mol of chlorine. Calculate the value of K_c for this decomposition into PCl_3 and Cl_2.

	PCl_5	$\rightleftharpoons$	PCl_3	$+$	Cl_2
Initial concentration	$\dfrac{1.33}{V}$		0		0
Equilibrium concentration	$\dfrac{1.33 - x}{15}$		$\dfrac{x}{15}$		$\dfrac{x}{15}$

The value of x is 0.8 because this is the number of moles of chlorine in the equilibrium mixture (this is given in the question). V is 15 dm³ and is the total volume of the equilibrium mixture. In this calculation, where the number of reactant particles does not equal the number of product particles, V does not cancel.

$$[PCl_5] = \frac{1.33 - 0.8}{15} = 0.035$$

$$[PCl_3] = \frac{0.8}{15} = 0.053$$

$$[Cl_2] = \frac{0.8}{15} = 0.053$$

$$K_c = \frac{[PCl_3][Cl_2]}{[PCl_5]} = \frac{0.053 \times 0.053}{0.035} = 0.08 \, \text{mol} \, \text{dm}^{-3}$$

Changing the conditions of an equilibrium reaction

The qualitative effect of changing the reaction conditions can be predicted by using **Le Chatelier's principle**. This principle states that 'a system at equilibrium will react to oppose any change imposed upon it'.

Example 1: changing concentration

The Haber process can be used as an example:

$N_2(g) + 3H_2(g) \rightleftharpoons 2NH_3(g)$

- If the concentration of either reactant N_2 or H_2 is increased, then the position of the equilibrium is displaced to the right (so as to reduce the concentration of N_2 or H_2). This means that more NH_3 is obtained.
- If the product NH_3 is removed, the position of the equilibrium is also displaced to the right to replace the NH_3.
- If the product NH_3 is added, the equilibrium position shifts to the left to remove the NH_3.
- The equilibrium constant K_c is unchanged, since there is no change in temperature.

Example 2: the effect of a change in total pressure

The steam re-forming of methane can be used as an example:

$$CH_4(g) + H_2O(g) \rightleftharpoons 3H_2(g) + CO(g)$$

- Changes in total pressure only have a significant effect on equilibrium reactions involving gases.
- An increase in total pressure displaces the equilibrium to the side of the equation that has the fewer moles of gas.
- In this example, there are 2 moles of gaseous reactants and 4 moles of gaseous products. Moving in the forward direction leads to an increase in the pressure because the number of moles increases from 2 to 4. Therefore, increasing the pressure shifts the equilibrium position to the left.
- Changing the pressure has no effect on the equilibrium constant K_c.

Example 3: the effect of a change in temperature

The decomposition of dinitrogen tetraoxide can be used as an example. This reaction is endothermic in the forward direction.

$$N_2O_4(g) \rightleftharpoons 2NO_2(g) \qquad \Delta H = +58\,kJ\,mol^{-1}$$

- If the temperature is increased, the equilibrium responds and tries to reduce the temperature.
- The equilibrium position shifts to the right and more NO_2 is produced.
- The value of K_c increases.

If the enthalpy change for the reaction is negative, then the reaction is exothermic and the forward direction leads to an increase in temperature.

- If the temperature is increased, the position of the equilibrium shifts to oppose the change and reduce the temperature.
- For a reaction that is exothermic in the forward direction, an increase in temperature shifts the position of the equilibrium to the left and there is less product in the equilibrium mixture.
- The value of K_c decreases.

Example 4: the addition of a catalyst

- The addition of a catalyst to a mixture at equilibrium has no effect on the composition of the equilibrium mixture.
- A catalyst speeds up the rates of the forward and backward reactions equally.
- A catalyst has no effect on the equilibrium position or on the value of the equilibrium constant, but the rate at which equilibrium is achieved is increased.

Equilibrium constant, K_p, for homogeneous reactions

In gaseous systems, the amount of gas in the system is usually given by the **partial pressure**. The partial pressure of a gas is the mole fraction of the gas present multiplied by the total pressure.

For example, if two gases, A and B, are present in a system and the total pressure is P_T, then the partial pressure of gas A is given by the expression:

partial pressure of gas A = mole fraction of gas A × total pressure

$$p_A = x_A \times P_T$$

partial pressure of gas B = mole fraction of gas B × total pressure

$$p_B = x_B \times P_T$$

The **mole fraction** is defined as the number of moles of a particular gas divided by the total number of moles of gas.

$$\text{mole fraction of gas A} = \frac{\text{moles of gas A}}{\text{total moles of gas}}$$

$$\text{mole fraction of gas B} = \frac{\text{moles of gas B}}{\text{total moles of gas}}$$

Example

Two gases, A and B, exist in equilibrium. There are 4 moles of A and 6 moles of B, so the total number of moles of gas is 10. The total pressure is 1.01 kPa. Deduce the mole fractions of A and B and deduce the partial pressures of A and B.

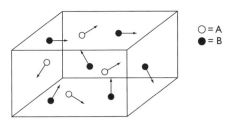

$$\text{mole fraction of A} = \frac{4}{10} = 0.4$$

$$\text{mole fraction of B} = \frac{6}{10} = 0.6$$

partial pressure of A = 0.4 × 1.01 = 0.404 kPa

partial pressure of B = 0.6 × 1.01 = 0.606 kPa

Check Add the partial pressures together; they should always equal the total pressure, that is, 0.404 + 0.606 = 1.01 kPa.

The equilibrium constant, K_p, is calculated from partial pressures, p, at constant temperature. For the following reaction:

$$aA(g) + bB(g) \rightleftharpoons cC(g) + dD(g)$$

$$K_p = \frac{p(C)^c p(D)^d}{p(A)^a p(B)^b}$$

Examples

The table below contains the expressions for K_p for some common equilibrium reactions. Note that partial pressures are shown by parentheses and not by square brackets.

Reaction	K_p	Units
$PCl_5 \rightleftharpoons PCl_3 + Cl_2$	$K_p = \dfrac{p(PCl_3)(pCl_2)}{p(PCl_5)}$	kPa
$N_2O_4 \rightleftharpoons 2NO_2$	$K_p = \dfrac{p(NO_2)^2}{p(N_2O_4)}$	kPa
$N_2 + 3H_2 \rightleftharpoons 2NH_3$	$K_p = \dfrac{p(NH_3)^2}{p(N_2)(pH_2)^3}$	kPa^{-2}
$2SO_2 + O_2 \rightleftharpoons 2SO_3$	$K_p = \dfrac{p(SO_3)^2}{p(SO_2)^2(pO_2)}$	kPa^{-1}

Calculations involving K_p

Example: the decomposition of phosphorus(V) chloride

2.5 mol of PCl_5 vapour was heated to 600 K in a sealed vessel. The equilibrium mixture at a pressure of 670 kPa contained 1.5 mol of chlorine gas. Calculate the value of the equilibrium constant K_p for the decomposition of PCl_5 into PCl_3 and Cl_2.

$$PCl_5 \rightleftharpoons PCl_3 + Cl_2$$

Initial moles	2.5	0	0
Equilibrium moles	2.5 − x	x	x	where x = 1.5
	= 1.0	1.5	1.5

total moles = 1.0 + 1.5 + 1.5 = 4.0
partial pressure = mole fraction × total pressure

partial pressure of $PCl_5 = \dfrac{1.0}{4.0} \times 670 = 167.5\,kPa$

partial pressure of $PCl_3 = \dfrac{1.5}{4.0} \times 670 = 251.25\,kPa$

partial pressure of $Cl_2 = \dfrac{1.5}{4.0} \times 670 = 251.25\,kPa$

Check The sum of the partial pressures should equal the total pressure, that is, 167.5 + 251.25 + 251.25 = 670 kPa.

$$K_p = \frac{p(PCl_3)p(Cl_2)}{p(PCl_5)} = \frac{251.25 \times 251.25}{167.5} = 377\,kPa$$

Acids and bases

You need to be able to:
- define acids and bases in terms of proton transfer
- define pH and carry out pH calculations for strong acids and bases

- define K_w and use this in the calculation of pH for strong bases
- understand the concept of weak acids and bases
- define K_a and pK_a and calculate pH, pK_a and K_a for weak acids
- understand the typical shape of pH curves for all combinations of weak and strong monoprotic acids and bases and be able to perform calculations for these titrations
- understand the shape of the pH curves for the titrations of sodium carbonate with HCl and of ethanedioic acid with NaOH
- define an indicator and select a suitable indicator for a particular titration curve
- explain the action of acidic and basic buffers and calculate the pH of buffer solutions

The Brønsted–Lowry theory of acids and bases

- An acid is a proton (H^+) donor.
- A base is a proton (H^+) acceptor.
- Acid–base equilibria involve the transfer of protons.

Example 1: an acid with water
The acid HA reacts with water to produce the following equilibrium:

$$HA \ + \ H_2O \ \rightleftharpoons \ A^- \ + \ H_3O^+$$
$$\text{acid} \quad \text{base} \qquad \text{base} \quad \text{acid}$$

Example 2: a base with water
The base A^- reacts with water to produce the following equilibrium:

$$A^- \ + \ H_2O \ \rightleftharpoons \ HA \ + \ OH^-$$
$$\text{base} \quad \text{acid} \qquad \text{acid} \quad \text{base}$$

You might be asked to complete equations and label the species as acids or bases. Common examples include the following:

$$HCl \ + \ H_2O \ \rightleftharpoons \ H_3O^+ \ + \ Cl^-$$
$$\text{acid} \quad \text{base} \qquad \text{acid} \quad \text{base}$$

$$NH_3 \ + \ H_2O \ \rightleftharpoons \ NH_4^+ \ + \ OH^-$$
$$\text{base} \quad \text{acid} \qquad \text{acid} \quad \text{base}$$

$$CH_3COOH \ + \ NH_3 \ \rightleftharpoons \ CH_3COO^- \ + \ NH_4^+$$
$$\text{acid} \qquad \text{base} \qquad \text{base} \qquad \text{acid}$$

$$HNO_3 \ + \ H_2SO_4 \ \rightleftharpoons \ H_2NO_3^+ \ + \ HSO_4^-$$
$$\text{base} \qquad \text{acid} \qquad \text{acid} \qquad \text{base}$$

The definition and calculation of pH

The acidity of an aqueous solution depends upon the number of $H^+(aq)$ ions in solution.

- pH is defined by the equation:
  $$pH = -\log_{10} [H^+]$$
  where $[H^+]$ is in mol dm^{-3}.
- Acid strength depends on the molar concentration of H$^+$ ions: the greater the concentration of H$^+$ ions, the lower the pH and the greater the acid strength.
- When calculating the pH of a strong acid (e.g. HCl, HNO$_3$, H$_2$SO$_4$) or a strong base (e.g. NaOH, KOH) complete dissociation is always assumed.

A similar relationship exists for a strong base, the strength of the base being dependent on the number of OH$^-$ ions in solution.
- pOH can be defined by the equation:
  $$pOH = -\log_{10} [OH^-]$$
- The pH of a strong base at 298 K can be calculated using the relationship:
  $$pH + pOH = 14$$

Examples
(1) Calculate the pH of an aqueous solution of 0.1 mol dm^{-3} HCl.

Assuming complete dissociation, 0.1 mol dm^{-3} HCl gives 0.1 mol dm^{-3} H$^+$ ions.
$$pH = -\log_{10} [H^+] = -\log_{10} 0.1 = 1$$
(2) Calculate the pH of an aqueous solution of 0.1 mol dm^{-3} NaOH.

Assuming complete dissociation, 0.1 mol dm^{-3} NaOH gives 0.1 mol dm^{-3} OH$^-$ ions.
$$pOH = -\log_{10} [OH^-] = -\log_{10} 0.1 = 1$$
$$pOH + pH = 14$$
$$pH = 14 - 1 = 13$$
(3) Calculate the concentration of H$^+$ ions given that the pH of a solution of HCl is 2.50.
$$pH = -\log_{10} [H^+], \text{ so } [H^+] = 10^{-pH}$$
$$[H^+] = 10^{-2.5} = 3.16 \times 10^{-3} \text{ mol dm}^{-3}$$

The ionic product of water, K_w

Water can act as both an acid (a proton donor) and a base (a proton acceptor). As a result, both H$_3$O$^+$ ions and OH$^-$ ions can exist simultaneously in water.
$$H_2O + H_2O \rightleftharpoons H_3O^+ + OH^-$$

This equilibrium can be represented more simply as:
$$H_2O(l) \rightleftharpoons H^+(aq) + OH^-(aq)$$

The equilibrium constant, K_c, for this reaction is:
$$K_c = \frac{[H^+][OH^-]}{[H_2O]}$$

The amount of water that dissociates is incredibly small and the equilibrium lies well over to the left-hand side. The concentration of water can be treated as a constant and incorporated into the value of K_c. This produces a new constant called the ionic product of water (symbol K_w).
$$K_w = [H^+][OH^-] = 1 \times 10^{-14} \text{ mol}^2 \text{ dm}^{-6} \text{ at } 298 \text{ K}$$

The value of K_w increases with an increase in temperature. This is because the dissociation of water is an endothermic reaction (+57 kJ mol⁻¹). (The opposite reaction, the neutralisation of an acid and a base, is an exothermic process.)

Examples

(1) Calculate the pH of water at 373 K (K_w = 51.3 × 10⁻¹⁴ at 373 K).

$K_w = [H^+][OH^-] = 51.3 \times 10^{-14}$

Assuming $[H^+] = [OH^-]$, then $[H^+]^2 = 51.3 \times 10^{-14}$

$[H^+] = \sqrt{51.3 \times 10^{-14}} = 7.16 \times 10^{-7}$

$pH = -\log_{10} (7.16 \times 10^{-7}) = 6.14$

(2) Calculate the pH of a 0.1 mol dm⁻³ solution of sodium hydroxide.

$K_w = [H^+][OH^-] = 1 \times 10^{-14} \, mol^2 \, dm^{-6}$

$[H^+] = \dfrac{K_w}{[OH^-]} = \dfrac{1 \times 10^{-14}}{0.1} = 1 \times 10^{-13} \, mol \, dm^{-3}$

$pH = -\log_{10} [H^+] = -\log_{10} (1 \times 10^{-13}) = 13$

(3) An aqueous solution of potassium hydroxide has a pH of 12.90. Calculate the molar concentration of the potassium hydroxide solution.

$pH = -\log_{10} [H^+]$, so $[H^+] = 10^{-pH}$

$[H^+] = 10^{-12.9} = 1.26 \times 10^{-13} \, mol \, dm^{-3}$

$[OH^-] = \dfrac{K_w}{[H^+]} = \dfrac{1 \times 10^{-14}}{1.26 \times 10^{-13}} = 0.079 \, mol \, dm^{-3}$

Since KOH is a strong base, its concentration will also be 0.079 mol dm⁻³.

Weak acids and bases

A weak acid only partially dissociates in aqueous solution. An example of a weak acid is ethanoic acid, CH_3COOH.

$CH_3COOH(aq) \rightleftharpoons CH_3COO^-(aq) + H^+(aq)$

The amount of dissociation is indicated by the acid dissociation constant, K_a.

$K_a = \dfrac{[CH_3COO^-][H^+]}{[CH_3COOH]} = 1.7 \times 10^{-5} \, mol \, dm^{-3}$

The larger the K_a value of an acid, the greater the dissociation of the acid and the stronger the acid.

- HF, with a K_a value of 5.6 × 10⁻⁴ mol dm⁻³, is a stronger acid than ethanoic acid.
- HCN, with a K_a value of 4.9 × 10⁻¹⁰ mol dm⁻³, is a weaker acid than ethanoic acid.

A weak base only partially dissociates in aqueous solution. An example of a weak base is ammonia, NH_3.

$NH_3 + H_2O \rightleftharpoons NH_4^+(aq) + OH^-(aq)$

K_b is small because ammonia is a weak base.

$K_b = \dfrac{[NH_4^+][OH^-]}{[NH_3]} = 1.7 \times 10^{-5} \, mol \, dm^{-3}$

Calculating the pH of a weak acid

Using the equation for the dissociation of a weak acid it can be seen that the number of moles of H^+ ions produced is always the same as the number of moles of CH_3COO^- ions produced, so the top line of the K_a expression becomes $[H^+]^2$. For weak acids it can be assumed that the amount of dissociation is so small that the concentration of the CH_3COOH at equilibrium is the same as the original concentration of CH_3COOH.

Example

Calculate the pH of a $0.1 \, mol \, dm^{-3}$ solution of ethanoic acid ($K_a = 1.7 \times 10^{-5}$).

$$1.7 \times 10^{-5} = \frac{[CH_3COO^-][H^+]}{[CH_3COOH]} = \frac{[H^+]^2}{[CH_3COOH]_{original}} = \frac{[H^+]^2}{0.1}$$

$$[H^+]^2 = 0.1 \times 1.7 \times 10^{-5} = 1.7 \times 10^{-6}$$

$$\therefore \quad [H^+] = \sqrt{1.7 \times 10^{-6}} = 1.304 \times 10^{-3}$$

$$pH = -\log_{10}(1.304 \times 10^{-3}) = 2.88$$

The definition of pK_a

Acid strength can also be defined by the term pK_a, where $pK_a = -\log_{10} K_a$.

Consider the following K_a and pK_a values:

Acid A	$K_a = 1 \times 10^{-5}$	$pK_a = 5$
Acid B	$K_a = 1 \times 10^{-3}$	$pK_a = 3$

The stronger acid will dissociate more, leading to a larger K_a value and a smaller pK_a value. Acid B is stronger than acid A. For example, chloroethanoic acid ($ClCH_2COOH$) has a pK_a value of 2.85, so it has a K_a value of $10^{-2.85}$, which is $1.41 \times 10^{-3} \, mol \, dm^{-3}$.

pH curves, titrations and indicators

pH curves

A graph of the pH of a solution being titrated against the volume of solution added is known as a pH curve. The **equivalence point** (or stoichiometric point) occurs when stoichiometrically equivalent amounts of acid and base have been added together. The **end point** of the titration is the point at which the indicator changes colour. The equivalence point can be determined accurately with an indicator when the end point coincides with the equivalence point. An indicator is suitable if the rapid change of pH at equivalence (shown by the near-vertical portion on the pH curve) overlaps the range of activity of the indicator.

The following pH curves are for various combinations of $0.1 \, mol \, dm^{-3}$ solutions of acids and bases. The ranges of two common indicators, phenolphthalein (range = 8.3–10.0) and methyl orange (range = 3.2–4.4), are shown to demonstrate their suitability. Summaries are provided for each titration curve. You need to be able to sketch these curves. Always remember to label the axes. The symbols used on the pH curves are EP (equivalence point), PP (phenolphthalein) and MO (methyl orange).

Addition of a strong base to a strong acid

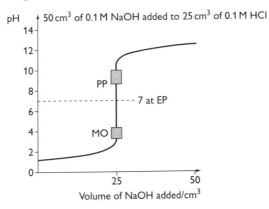

50 cm³ of 0.1 M NaOH added to 25 cm³ of 0.1 M HCl

$$HCl + NaOH \longrightarrow NaCl + H_2O$$

- The pH starts at 1 and rises slowly.
- There is a rapid change in pH just before the equivalence point.
- The pH is 7 at the equivalence point.
- The pH is 12.5 after adding 50 cm³ of NaOH.
- Either methyl orange or phenolphthalein could be used to show the equivalence point.

Addition of a strong base to a weak acid

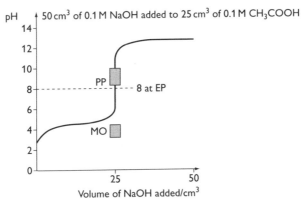

50 cm³ of 0.1 M NaOH added to 25 cm³ of 0.1 M CH₃COOH

$$CH_3COOH + NaOH \longrightarrow CH_3COONa + H_2O$$

- The pH starts at 3 and rises slowly.
- There is a rapid change in pH just before the equivalence point.
- The pH is 8 at the equivalence point due to the presence of OH⁻ ions in solution.
$$CH_3COO^- + H_2O \rightleftharpoons CH_3COOH + OH^-$$
- The pH is 12.5 after adding 50 cm³ of NaOH.
- Phenolphthalein can be used to indicate the equivalence point; methyl orange is not suitable.

Addition of a weak base to a strong acid

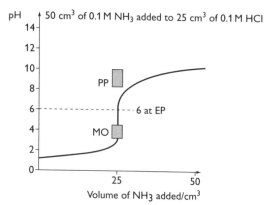

$$HCl + NH_3 \longrightarrow NH_4Cl$$

- The pH starts at 1 and rises slowly.
- There is a rapid change in pH just before the equivalence point.
- The pH is 6 at the equivalence point due to the presence of H^+ ions in solution.
$$NH_4^+ + H_2O \rightleftharpoons NH_3 + H_3O^+$$
- The pH is 11 after adding 50 cm^3 of NH_3.
- Methyl orange can be used to indicate the equivalence point; phenolphthalein is not suitable.

Addition of a weak base to a weak acid

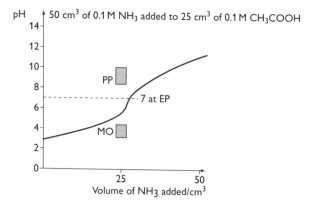

$$CH_3COOH + NH_3 \longrightarrow CH_3COO^- + NH_4^+$$

- The pH starts at 3 and rises gradually.
- The variation of pH with volume near the end point is too gradual for the detection of the equivalence point.
- The pH is 7 at the equivalence point.
- The pH is 11 after adding 50 cm^3 NH_3.
- Neither methyl orange nor phenolphthalein is suitable.

Using a pH curve to determine pK_a and K_a for a weak acid

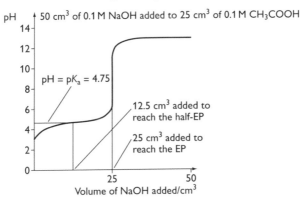

50 cm³ of 0.1 M NaOH added to 25 cm³ of 0.1 M CH₃COOH

The pH curve for a weak acid and a strong base can be used to determine pK_a. If the volume needed for the equivalence point is 25 cm³, then the half-equivalence point occurs at 12.5 cm³. This is the point when only half the acid has been neutralised. At this point $[CH_3COOH] = [CH_3COO^-]$, so the expression for K_a can be simplified.

$$K_a = \frac{[CH_3COO^-][H^+]}{[CH_3COOH]}$$

$K_a = [H^+]$, so $pK_a = pH$

Reading from the graph, the pH = 4.75, so pK_a = 4.75 and K_a is 1.78×10^{-5} mol dm⁻³.

Two-indicator titrations

Titration of 0.1 M sodium carbonate with 0.1 M hydrochloric acid

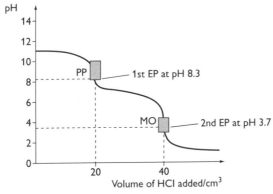

In this reaction, 50 cm³ of 0.1 mol dm⁻³ HCl is added to 20 cm³ of a 0.1 mol dm⁻³ solution of sodium carbonate. There are two stages to this reaction, which correspond to two equivalence points at 20 cm³ and 40 cm³.

$$Na_2CO_3 + HCl \longrightarrow NaHCO_3 + NaCl$$
$$NaHCO_3 + HCl \longrightarrow NaCl + CO_2 + H_2O$$

These stages can be represented by ionic equations:

$$CO_3^{2-} + H^+ \longrightarrow HCO_3^-$$
$$HCO_3^- + H^+ \longrightarrow H_2CO_3 \longrightarrow H_2O + CO_2$$

- The pH starts at 11 and decreases slowly, then there is a rapid change just before the first equivalence point.
- The pH is 8.3 at the first equivalence point, so it can be detected by phenolphthalein.
- The pH curve flattens out, then there is a rapid change just before the second equivalence point.
- The pH is 3.7 at the second equivalence point, so it can be detected by methyl orange.
- The pH is 2 when 50 cm³ of HCl has been added.

Titration of ethanedioic acid and sodium hydroxide

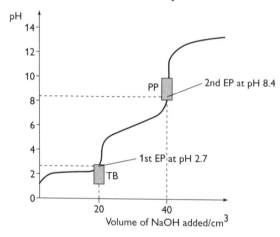

In this reaction, 50 cm³ of 0.1 mol dm⁻³ NaOH are added to 20 cm³ of a 0.1 mol dm⁻³ solution of ethanedioic acid. There are two stages to this reaction, which correspond to two equivalence points at 20 cm³ and 40 cm³.

$$HOOC-COOH + NaOH \longrightarrow NaOOC-COOH + H_2O$$
$$NaOOC-COOH + NaOH \longrightarrow NaOOC-COONa + H_2O$$

These stages can be represented by ionic equations:

$$HOOC-COOH + OH^- \longrightarrow {}^-OOC-COOH + H_2O$$
$${}^-OOC-COOH + OH^- \longrightarrow {}^-OOC-COO^- + H_2O$$

- The pH starts at approximately 1 and increases gradually, then there is a rapid change just before the first equivalence point.
- The pH is 2.7 at the first equivalence point, so thymol blue (TB, range = 1.2–2.8) is a better indicator than methyl orange.
- The pH curve flattens out, then there is a rapid change just before the second equivalence point.
- The pH is 8.4 at the second equivalence point, so it is detected by phenolphthalein.
- The pH is 12.5 when 50 cm³ of NaOH has been added.

Indicators

An acid–base indicator is a water-soluble weak organic acid. The acid and base forms of the indicator have different colours and the colour changes over a narrow pH range.

Phenolphthalein has the following structure:

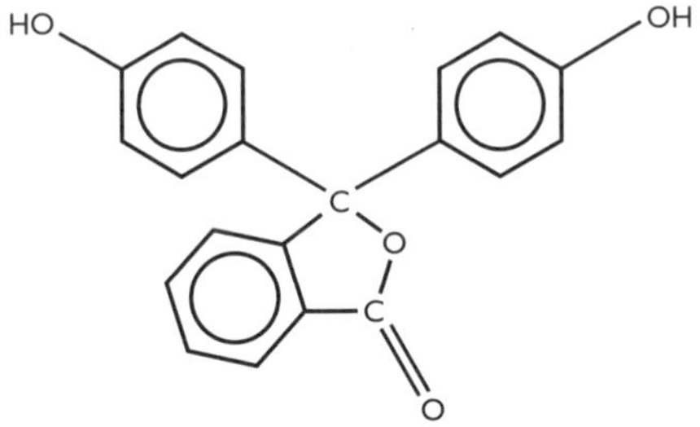

It is colourless in acidic conditions (low pH). This structure, which exists in acidic conditions, can be simplified as HIn. Phenolphthalein is pink in alkaline conditions (high pH) and its structure can be simplified as In⁻. These forms exist in the following equilibrium:

$$HIn \rightleftharpoons In^- + H^+$$

colourless   pink

At the equivalence point of an acid–base titration, the pH changes rapidly through several units of pH. The above equilibrium swings from almost all HIn to virtually all In⁻, so the colour changes from colourless to pink. This colour change is used to indicate the end point of the titration. If it coincides with the rapid change of pH at the equivalence point, then the indicator is suitable for use in the titration.

An indicator is a weak acid. Its dissociation is described by the expression:

$$K_{in} = \frac{[H^+][In^-]}{[HIn]}$$

At the end point, $[HIn] = [In^-]$, so $K_{in} = [H^+]$. This means that $pK_{in} = pH$ at the end point. The pK_{in} for phenolphthalein = 9.3, and its range of use covers pH 8.3–10.0.

Different indicators are used because they cover different ranges of pH.

Indicator	pK$_{in}$	pH range	Colour in acid	Colour in alkali
Thymol blue	1.7	1.2–2.8	Red	Yellow
Methyl orange	3.7	3.2–4.4	Red	Yellow
Methyl red	5.1	4.2–6.3	Red	Yellow
Bromothymol blue	7.0	6.0–7.6	Yellow	Blue
Phenol red	7.9	6.8–8.4	Yellow	Red
Phenolphthalein	9.3	8.3–10.0	Colourless	Pink
Thymolphthalein	9.7	9.3–10.5	Colourless	Blue

Calculations and titrations

Example 1: concentrations and volumes

$13.3\,cm^3$ of a solution of NaOH was required to neutralise $20.0\,cm^3$ of a $0.08\,mol\,dm^{-3}$ solution of H_2SO_4. Calculate the concentration of the NaOH solution.

$$2NaOH + H_2SO_4 \longrightarrow Na_2SO_4 + 2H_2O$$

$$\text{moles of } H_2SO_4 = \frac{MV}{1000}$$

$$= \frac{0.08 \times 20}{1000} = 1.6 \times 10^{-3}$$

From the equation, 2 moles NaOH react with 1 mole H_2SO_4.

moles of NaOH in $13.3\,cm^3 = 2 \times 1.6 \times 10^{-3} = 3.2 \times 10^{-3}$

$$\text{moles of NaOH in } 1000\,cm^3 = \frac{3.2 \times 10^{-3} \times 1000}{13.3} = 0.24\,mol\ NaOH$$

concentration of NaOH $= 0.24\,mol\,dm^{-3}$

Example 2: finding the pH during a strong acid–strong base titration

- Calculate the number of moles of acid using $\frac{MV}{1000}$.
- Calculate the number of moles of base using $\frac{MV}{1000}$.
- Calculate the number of moles of excess acid (or excess base).
- Find the total volume of solution produced by the mixture (acid + base).
- Determine the concentration of excess acid (or base) in $mol\,dm^{-3}$.
- Determine the pH using $pH = -\log_{10}[H^+]$.
- Use $K_w = [H^+][OH^-]$ if calculating the pH of a base.

Calculate the pH during a titration when $20.0\,cm^3$ of a $0.10\,mol\,dm^{-3}$ solution of NaOH were added to $25.0\,cm^3$ of $0.15\,mol\,dm^{-3}$ HCl.

$$\text{moles of HCl} = \frac{MV}{1000} = \frac{0.15 \times 25}{1000} = 3.75 \times 10^{-3}$$

$$\text{moles of NaOH} = \frac{MV}{1000} = \frac{0.1 \times 20}{1000} = 2.0 \times 10^{-3}$$

moles of excess HCl $= (3.75 \times 10^{-3}) - (2.0 \times 10^{-3}) = 1.75 \times 10^{-3}$

total volume of the solution $= 20 + 25 = 45\,cm^3$

$$\text{molar concentration of } H^+ = \frac{1.75 \times 10^{-3} \times 1000}{45} = 0.0389\,mol\,dm^{-3}$$

$pH = -\log_{10}[H^+] = -\log_{10}0.0389 = 1.41$

Example 3: finding the pH during a weak acid–strong base titration

The method depends on how far the titration has progressed.

Example 3a: before equivalence

The relative proportions of the weak acid and its anion have to be determined and the values used in the expression for K_a.

Calculate the pH in a titration when 10.0 cm^3 of 0.20 mol dm^{-3} solution of NaOH has been added to 25.0 cm^3 of a 0.25 mol dm^{-3} solution of ethanoic acid ($K_a = 1.76 \times 10^{-5} \text{ mol dm}^{-3}$).

$$CH_3COOH + NaOH \longrightarrow CH_3COONa + H_2O$$

or more simply:

$$CH_3COOH + OH^- \rightleftharpoons CH_3COO^- + H_2O$$

original moles of $CH_3COOH = \dfrac{MV}{1000} = \dfrac{0.25 \times 25}{1000} = 6.25 \times 10^{-3}$

moles of NaOH added $= \dfrac{MV}{1000} = \dfrac{0.2 \times 10}{1000} = 2.0 \times 10^{-3}$

moles of CH_3COO^- formed $= 2.0 \times 10^{-3}$

moles of CH_3COOH remaining $= (6.25 \times 10^{-3}) - (2 \times 10^{-3}) = 4.25 \times 10^{-3}$

Since the ethanoic acid and the ethanoate ions exist together in the same overall volume, the ratio of the concentrations is equal to the ratio of the number of moles.

$$K_a = \frac{[CH_3COO^-][H^+]}{[CH_3COOH]}$$

so $[H^+] = K_a \times \dfrac{[CH_3COOH]}{[CH_3COO^-]}$

$[H^+] = 1.76 \times 10^{-5} \times \dfrac{4.25 \times 10^{-3}}{2.0 \times 10^{-3}} = 3.74 \times 10^{-5} \text{ mol dm}^{-3}$

$pH = -\log_{10}[H^+] = -\log_{10}(3.74 \times 10^{-5}) = 4.43$

Example 3b: after equivalence

The excess of the strong base has to be found, together with the total volume of the solution. The molar concentration of the OH^- ions is then determined and the pH of the strong base is calculated using $K_w = [H^+][OH^-]$ and $pH = -\log_{10} [H^+]$.

Calculate the pH in a titration when 38.0 cm^3 of a 0.15 mol dm^{-3} solution of NaOH has been added to 20.0 cm^3 of a 0.20 mol dm^{-3} solution of ethanoic acid ($K_a = 1.76 \times 10^{-5} \text{ mol dm}^{-3}$).

$$CH_3COOH + NaOH \longrightarrow CH_3COONa + H_2O$$

moles of $CH_3COOH = \dfrac{MV}{1000} = \dfrac{0.20 \times 20}{1000} = 4.0 \times 10^{-3}$

moles of NaOH added $= \dfrac{MV}{1000} = \dfrac{0.15 \times 38}{1000} = 5.7 \times 10^{-3}$

moles of excess NaOH $= (5.7 \times 10^{-3}) - (4.0 \times 10^{-3}) = 1.7 \times 10^{-3}$

total volume of solution $= 20 \text{ cm}^3 + 38 \text{ cm}^3 = 58 \text{ cm}^3$

concentration of NaOH $= \dfrac{1.7 \times 10^{-3} \times 1000}{58} = 2.93 \times 10^{-2}$

$[H^+] = \dfrac{K_w}{[OH^-]} = \dfrac{1 \times 10^{-14}}{2.93 \times 10^{-2}} = 3.41 \times 10^{-13}$

$pH = -\log_{10}[H^+] = -\log_{10}(3.41 \times 10^{-13}) = 12.47$

Buffer solutions

A buffer is a solution that resists changes in pH when small amounts of acid or base are added. A buffer solution is also able to maintain its pH on dilution.

Acidic buffers

An acidic buffer maintains a constant pH at a pH below 7. It is a mixture of a weak acid and its conjugate base, for example ethanoic acid (CH_3COOH) and sodium ethanoate (CH_3COONa).

In this buffer solution there is:
- a large amount of undissociated ethanoic acid, because it is a weak acid
- a large amount of ethanoate ions, owing to the addition of sodium ethanoate which completely ionises in solution

This gives the following equilibrium:

$$CH_3COOH \rightleftharpoons CH_3COO^- + H^+$$

large amount   large amount

- On addition of a small amount of acid, the equilibrium will be driven to the left-hand side to remove the H^+ ions, thus maintaining the pH.
- On addition of a small amount of alkali, the OH^- ions will react with the H^+ ions to form H_2O. The equilibrium will be driven to the right-hand side to replace the H^+ ions, thus maintaining the pH.

Basic buffers

A basic buffer maintains a constant pH at a pH above 7. It is a mixture of a weak base and its conjugate acid, for example ammonia (NH_3) and ammonium chloride (NH_4Cl).

In this buffer solution there is:
- a large amount of undissociated ammonia, because it is a weak base
- a large amount of ammonium ions, owing to the addition of ammonium chloride which completely ionises in solution

This gives the following equilibrium:

$$NH_3 + H_2O \rightleftharpoons NH_4^+ + OH^-$$

large amount   large amount

- On addition of a small amount of acid, the H^+ ions will react with the OH^- ions to form H_2O. The equilibrium will be driven to the right-hand side to replace the OH^- ions, thus maintaining the pH.
- On addition of a small amount of alkali, the equilibrium will be driven to the left-hand side to remove the OH^- ions, thus maintaining the pH.

Dilution of a buffer solution

The expression for K_a for ethanoic acid is:

$$K_a = \frac{[CH_3COO^-][H^+]}{[CH_3COOH]}$$

Rearranging gives:

$$[H^+] = K_a \frac{[CH_3COOH]}{[CH_3COO^-]}$$

On dilution, the concentrations of CH_3COOH and CH_3COO^- will change by the same amount. The concentration of H^+ will not change, so the pH will remain constant.

Calculating the pH of an acidic buffer solution

Consider the buffer solution formed when ethanoic acid and sodium ethanoate are mixed together.

$$CH_3COOH \rightleftharpoons CH_3COO^- + H^+$$

Calculate the pH of a buffer solution made by mixing $15\,cm^3$ of $1.0\,mol\,dm^{-3}$ solution of ethanoic acid ($K_a = 1.76 \times 10^{-5}\,mol\,dm^{-3}$) with $18\,cm^3$ of $0.8\,mol\,dm^{-3}$ solution of sodium ethanoate.

$$K_a = \frac{[CH_3COO^-][H^+]}{[CH_3COOH]}$$

$$[H^+] = K_a \frac{[CH_3COOH]}{[CH_3COO^-]}$$

$$\text{moles of ethanoate} = \frac{0.8 \times 18}{1000} = 1.44 \times 10^{-2}$$

$$\text{moles of ethanoic acid} = \frac{1.0 \times 15}{1000} = 1.5 \times 10^{-2}$$

$$[H^+] = 1.76 \times 10^{-5} \times \frac{1.5 \times 10^{-2}}{1.44 \times 10^{-2}} = 1.83 \times 10^{-5}$$

$$pH = -\log_{10}[H^+] = -\log_{10}(1.83 \times 10^{-5}) = 4.74$$

Nomenclature and isomerism in organic chemistry

You need to be able to apply the International Union of Pure and Applied Chemistry (IUPAC) rules for nomenclature to simple organic compounds, limited to chains with up to six carbon atoms and containing the functional groups listed below:

alkanes	alkenes	haloalkanes
alcohols	aldehydes	ketones
carboxylic acids	esters	acyl chlorides
acid anhydrides	amines	amides
amino acids	arenes	

You also need to understand the basic principles of structural isomerism and stereo-isomerism (geometric and optical).

Nomenclature

The modern name of an organic compound depends upon:
- the length of the main carbon chain
- the names of the functional groups and carbon side chains present
- the number and position of the functional groups and carbon side chains on the main carbon chain

Organic compounds are named according to the rules of IUPAC.

(1) The root of the name is derived from the number of carbon atoms present in the longest *unbranched* chain.

Number of carbon atoms	1	2	3	4	5	6	7	8
Root	Meth-	Eth-	Prop-	But-	Pent-	Hex-	Hept-	Oct-

$$H_3C\text{—}CH_2\text{—}CH_2\text{—}CH_2\text{—}CH_2\text{—}CH_3$$
Hexane

(2) If the carbon chain is joined up as a ring, then the prefix 'cyclo-' is used, for example 'cyclohex-' in cyclohexane.

Cyclohexane

(3) A chain can be saturated or unsaturated; this is indicated by the second part of the name. Saturated compounds contain '-an-', for example ethane, CH_3CH_3. Compounds with a carbon–carbon double bond contain '-en-', for example ethene, $CH_2=CH_2$.

(4) A prefix or suffix is used to indicate the presence of a functional group (see later). If no functional group is present then the name ends in the letter '-e'. For example, $CH_3CH_2CH_3$ is propane and $CH_3CH=CH_2$ is propene.

(5) The carbon skeleton in many organic compounds is branched. The names of the side chains depend on the number of carbon atoms in them. For example, CH_3- is methyl, CH_3CH_2- is ethyl, $CH_3CH_2CH_2-$ is propyl etc.

Methylpentane

$$H_3C\text{—}\overset{\overset{\displaystyle CH_3}{|}}{CH}\text{—}CH_3$$

Ethylpentane

$$H_3C\text{—}CH_2\text{—}\overset{\overset{\displaystyle CH_3}{\overset{|}{\underset{|}{CH_2}}}}{CH}\text{—}CH_2\text{—}CH_3$$

(6) A number indicates the position of the functional group or side chain on the main carbon skeleton.

OH
Butan-2-ol

H_3C—CH—CH_2—CH_3

(7) Carbon atoms are numbered consecutively from one end such that the attached groups are on the lowest-numbered carbon atoms.

H_3C—CH_2—CH_2—CH_2—OH
Butan-1-ol

(8) To indicate the position of a double bond, the number of the lowest-numbered carbon atom involved is placed before '-ene'.

H_2C=CH—CH_2—CH_2—CH_3
Pent-1-ene

(9) Aldehydes (–CHO), acids (–COOH) and nitriles (–CN) are always regarded as containing carbon number one.

CH_3

H_3C—CH—CH_2—C
3-methylbutanal   H
(with O and H groups shown)

Cl—CH_2—CH_2—C
3-chloropropanoic acid   OH

(10) If the same functional group appears more than once then this is indicated by a prefix. For example, for two groups use 'di-', for three groups use 'tri-', for four groups use 'tetra-' etc.

Br Br

H—C—C—CH_3
1,2-dibromopropane
H H

Cl H

Cl—C—C—H
1,1,1-trichloroethane
Cl H

(11) If more than one type of functional group is present then the names are listed in alphabetical order of the functional group. For example, 'bromo-' comes before 'chloro-' and 'tribromo-' comes before 'dichloro-'.

Br

H_3C—CH—CH_2—Cl
2-bromo-1-chloropropane

(12) When two names that usually end in suffixes are needed, the ending for acid takes precedence over aldehyde or ketone, which in turn take precedence over alcohol.

OH

H_3C—CH—C
2-hydroxypropanoic acid   OH

O

H_3C—C—CH_2—C
3-oxobutanoic acid   OH

(13) The suffix '-en' for alkenes can be placed in front of other suffixes. For example, '-enal' or '-enol'.

H H H

H_3C—C=C—C=O
But-2-enal

(14) Aromatic compounds contain benzene rings. Benzene rings with only one functional group are straightforward to name, e.g. nitrobenzene or chlorobenzene. When a benzene ring has more than one functional group, the groups are numbered around the ring in such a way that the lowest possible numbers are used. The functional groups are listed in alphabetical order, together with their appropriate numbers.

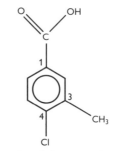

4-chloro-3-methylbenzenecarboxylic acid

Functional groups

Type of compound	Functional group	Suffix/prefix	Examples
Alkanes	$>C-H$	-ane	$H_3C - CH_3$ Ethane
Alkenes	$C=C$	-ene	$H_2C = CH_2$ Ethene
Haloalkanes	$-Cl, -Br, -I$	halo-	$H_3C - CH_2 - Cl$ Chloroethane
Alcohols	$-OH$	-ol	$H_3C - CH_2 - OH$ Ethanol
Ethers	$-OR$	alkoxy-	$H_3C - O - CH_3$ Methoxymethane
Aldehydes	$-C\overset{O}{\underset{H}{}}$	-al	$H_3C - C\overset{O}{\underset{H}{}}$ Ethanal
Ketones	$C=O$	-one	$\overset{O}{\underset{H_3C \quad CH_3}{C}}$ Propanone
Amines	$-NH_2$	amino- or -amine	$H_2N - CH_2 - C\overset{O}{\underset{OH}{}}$ Aminoethanoic acid $\quad$ $H_3C - NH_2$ Methylamine
Amides	$-C\overset{O}{\underset{NH_2}{}}$	-amide	$H_3C - C\overset{O}{\underset{NH_2}{}}$ Ethanamide
Nitriles	$-C\equiv N$	-nitrile	$H_3C - CH_2 - C\equiv N$ Propanenitrile

Type of compound	Functional group	Suffix/ prefix	Examples		
Esters	—C OR	-oate	Ethyl ethanoate		
Acyl halides	—C X = Cl, Br, I X	-oyl halide	Ethanoyl chloride		
Acid anhydrides		-oic anhydride	Ethanoic anhydride		
Aromatic		-benzene or phenyl-	Chlorobenzene	Methylbenzene Phenylamine	Phenylethene

Isomerism: structural isomers

Structural isomers are compounds with the same molecular formula but different structural formulae.

Chain isomerism

Chain isomerism occurs when there are two or more ways of arranging the carbon skeleton. These isomers have similar chemical properties but slightly different physical properties. The more branched the isomer, the weaker the van der Waals forces between different molecules, and so the boiling point is lower.

Example: isomers of C_4H_{10}

H_3C—CH_2—CH_2—CH_3
Butane

Methylpropane

Positional isomerism

Positional isomers have the same carbon skeleton and the same functional groups, but the functional groups are located at different places on the carbon skeleton.

Example: isomers of bromopropane

$$H_3C \text{---} CH_2 \text{---} CH_2 \text{---} Br$$
1-bromopropane

$$H_3C \text{---} CH \text{---} CH_3$$ with Br above the CH
2-bromopropane

Functional group isomerism

These isomers have different functional groups and so have different chemical and physical properties.

Example 1: aldehydes and ketones (C_3H_8O)

Propanal
$$H_3C \text{---} CH_2$$ ... $$C \text{===} O$$ ... H

Propanone
$$CH_3$$ ... $$C \text{===} O$$ ... CH_3

Example 2: alcohols and ethers (C_2H_6O)

$$H_3C \text{---} CH_2 \text{---} OH$$
Ethanol

$$H_3C \text{---} O \text{---} CH_3$$
Methoxymethane

Example 3: carboxylic acids and esters ($C_3H_6O_2$)

Propanoic acid
$$H_3C \text{---} CH_2 \text{---} C$$ with O (double bond) and OH

Methyl ethanoate
$$H_3C \text{---} C$$ with O (double bond) and $O \text{---} CH_3$

Ethyl methanoate
$$H \text{---} C$$ with O (double bond) and $O \text{---} CH_2 \text{---} CH_3$

Isomerism: stereoisomers

Compounds that have the same molecular and structural formula but a different spatial arrangement of their bonds are called stereoisomers.

Geometric isomerism

Geometric isomerism is also known as *cis–trans* isomerism. It is caused by the non-rotation of the carbon–carbon double bond in alkenes.

cis: Cl and Cl on top, H and H on bottom, $C \text{===} C$

trans: Cl (top left) and H (top right), H (bottom left) and Cl (bottom right), $C \text{===} C$

It is not possible to have geometrical isomers when there are two identical groups joined to the same carbon atom in a double bond.

Example: isomers of C₄H₈

There are three structural isomers of C_4H_8. Only one of these isomers exhibits geometric isomerism.

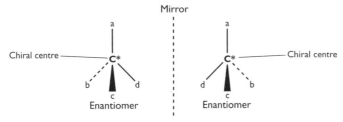

But-1-ene

trans-but-2-ene

Methylpropene

cis-but-2-ene

Optical isomerism

Compounds that possess a carbon atom with four different groups attached to it tetrahedrally exhibit optical isomerism because the asymmetric molecule cannot be superimposed on its mirror image.

Optically active compounds are called **chiral** compounds, with the asymmetric carbon atom known as the **chiral centre**. The two mirror images are stereoisomers, called **enantiomers**.

Mirror

Chiral centre — C*   C* — Chiral centre

Enantiomer   Enantiomer

Note the following:
- Enantiomers have the same molecular and structural formula and differ only in their spatial arrangement.
- They have the same physical and chemical properties except they rotate plane-polarised light in opposite directions.
- Mixing equal amounts of the two enantiomers gives an optically inactive mixture, which has no effect on plane-polarised light. This mixture is known as a **racemic mixture** or **racemate**.
- Many naturally occurring molecules exist as the single enantiomer, for example the amino acid alanine (2-aminopropanoic acid).
- Lactic acid (2-hydroxypropanoic acid), which is formed during the contraction of muscles, is optically active.
- Enzymes in the body are stereospecific and distinguish between enantiomers.

Example: lactic acid (2-hydroxypropanoic acid)

It has a carbon with four different groups attached, so it exhibits optical isomerism.

Compounds containing the carbonyl group

Aldehydes and ketones

You need to be able to recall the test to distinguish between aldehydes and ketones as well as the products, equations and mechanisms (using H⁻) for the reduction of aldehydes and ketones. You also need to understand the mechanism of nucleophilic addition for the reaction of carbonyl compounds with HCN to produce hydroxynitriles.

Nomenclature

Carbonyl compounds have the same general formula, $C_nH_{2n}O$, and contain the C=O group. Aldehydes have the C=O group at the end of the carbon chain while ketones have the C=O group elsewhere in the chain.

You need to be familiar with the naming of each type of carbonyl compound.

Aldehydes

Methanal   Ethanal   Propanal

H₃C — CH₂ — CH₂

C=O

H

Butanal

H

C — ⬡

O

Benzenecarbaldehyde

Ketones

O

C

H₃C   CH₃

Propanone

O

C

H₃C   CH₂ — CH₃

Butanone

H₃C — CH₂

C=O

H₃C — CH₂

Pentan-3-one

O

C

H₂C   CH₂

H₂C   CH₂

CH₂

Cyclohexanone

O

C — CH₃

⬡

Phenylethanone

Distinguishing between aldehydes and ketones

The tests depend upon the fact that aldehydes are stronger reducing agents than ketones. Aldehydes are easily oxidised to carboxylic acids but ketones are resistant to oxidation with mild oxidising agents.

Test 1: Tollens' reagent (the silver mirror test)
- **Reagents:** silver nitrate and ammonia solution
- **Procedure:** ammonia solution is added to silver nitrate until a brown precipitate of silver oxide forms and then dissolves to produce a colourless solution containing the complex $[Ag(NH_3)_2]^+$, which is added to the aldehyde. If there is no reaction, then the mixture is gently warmed.
- **Equation:** $CH_3CHO + [O] \longrightarrow CH_3COOH$
- **Observations:** an aldehyde is oxidised to a carboxylic acid and the silver complex is reduced to produce a metallic silver precipitate. A ketone gives no reaction.

Test 2: Fehling's solution
- **Reagents:** Fehling's A and B — a mixture of copper(II) sulphate solution (A) and sodium potassium tartrate in excess sodium hydroxide (B). These combine to produce a deep blue solution with a complex Cu^{2+} ion.
- **Procedure:** Fehling's solution is added to the test solution and the mixture is heated.
- **Equation:** $CH_3CHO + [O] \longrightarrow CH_3COOH$
- **Observations:** an aldehyde is oxidised to a carboxylic acid and the Cu^{2+} complex is reduced to a red precipitate of copper(I) oxide, Cu_2O. A ketone gives no reaction.

Test 3: potassium dichromate(VI) solution
- **Reagents:** potassium dichromate(VI) and dilute sulphuric acid
- **Equation:** $CH_3CHO + [O] \longrightarrow CH_3COOH$
- **Observations:** an aldehyde is oxidised to a carboxylic acid and the acidified potassium dichromate(VI) changes from orange to green. A ketone gives no reaction. (Remember that primary and secondary alcohols will also react with this reagent.)

Preparation of carbonyl compounds

The oxidation of primary alcohols produces aldehydes. For example:

$$CH_3CH_2OH + [O] \longrightarrow CH_3CHO + H_2O$$
$$\text{Ethanol} \qquad\qquad \text{Ethanal}$$

The reagents needed are acidified potassium dichromate(VI) and dilute H_2SO_4. The low boiling point aldehyde is collected under distillation.

The oxidation of secondary alcohols produces ketones. For example:

$$CH_3CH(OH)CH_3 + [O] \longrightarrow CH_3COCH_3 + H_2O$$
$$\text{Propan-2-ol} \qquad\qquad \text{Propanone}$$

The reagents needed are acidified potassium dichromate(VI) and dilute H_2SO_4. The reaction is carried out under reflux.

The reduction of carbonyl compounds

Reduction of aldehydes to primary alcohols
- **Reagent:** sodium tetrahydridoborate(III), $NaBH_4$
- **Conditions:** reflux in aqueous ethanol
- **Example:** butanal is reduced to butan-1-ol
- **Equation:** $CH_3CH_2CH_2CHO + 2[H] \longrightarrow CH_3CH_2CH_2CH_2OH$

or

- **Reagent:** hydrogen
- **Conditions:** heat and a nickel catalyst
- **Equation:** $CH_3CH_2CH_2CHO + H_2 \longrightarrow CH_3CH_2CH_2CH_2OH$

Reduction of ketones to secondary alcohols
- **Reagent:** sodium tetrahydridoborate(III), $NaBH_4$
- **Conditions:** reflux in aqueous ethanol
- **Example:** butanone is reduced to butan-2-ol
- **Equation:** $CH_3CH_2COCH_3 + 2[H] \longrightarrow CH_3CH_2CH(OH)CH_3$

or

- **Reagent:** hydrogen
- **Conditions:** heat and a nickel catalyst
- **Equation:** $CH_3CH_2COCH_3 + H_2 \longrightarrow CH_3CH_2CH(OH)CH_3$

If a compound contains a carbonyl group (C=O) and an alkene group (C=C) then both groups will be reduced by hydrogen in the presence of a nickel catalyst. To reduce the carbonyl group only, use $NaBH_4$.

Using H$_2$: $CH_3CH=CHCHO + 2H_2 \longrightarrow CH_3CH_2CH_2CH_2OH$
Using NaBH$_4$: $CH_3CH=CHCHO + 2[H] \longrightarrow CH_3CH=CHCH_2OH$

Nucleophilic addition in carbonyl compounds

Carbonyl compounds are unsaturated and undergo addition reactions. The C=O bond is polar because the oxygen atom is more electronegative than the carbon atom. The carbon atom of the C=O bond is electron deficient and is susceptible to attack by nucleophiles (electron-pair donors).

Example 1: addition of hydrogen cyanide (HCN) to ethanal
- **Reagent:** HCN
- **Equation:** $CH_3CHO + HCN \longrightarrow CH_3CH(OH)CN$
- **Product:** 2-hydroxypropanenitrile (racemic mixture of two enantiomers)
- **Mechanism:**

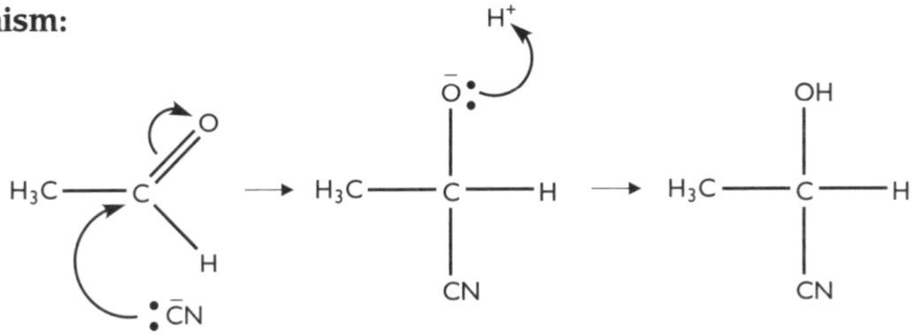

Example 2: addition of hydride ions (from NaBH$_4$) to ethanal
- **Reagent:** NaBH$_4$ (a source of H$^-$ ions), followed by dilute sulphuric acid
- **Equation:** $CH_3CHO + 2[H] \longrightarrow CH_3CH_2OH$
- **Product:** ethanol
- **Mechanism:**

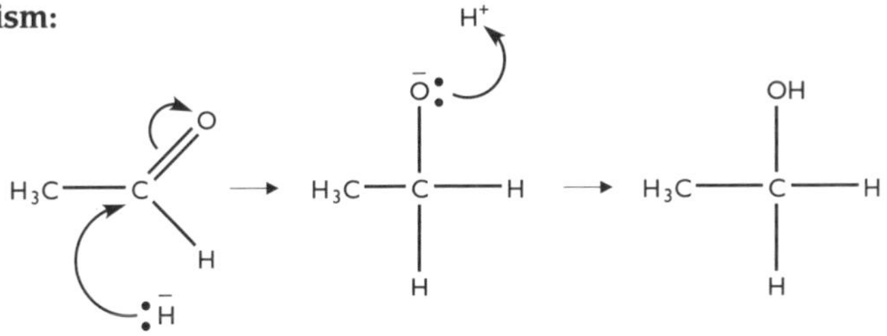

All other carbonyl compounds react in a similar fashion to ethanal and undergo nucleophilic addition reactions with HCN and NaBH$_4$. You need to be able to draw the mechanism for any carbonyl compound reacting with these reagents. The position of the curly arrows, to show electron pair movement, will always be the same. The only difference will be the structure of the carbonyl compound and the final product.

The importance of HCN reactions in synthetic routes
When carbonyl compounds undergo nucleophilic addition reactions with HCN the products formed contain the –CN group, which can:
- be readily hydrolysed by boiling in dilute hydrochloric acid to produce a carboxylic acid group, –COOH
   $CH_3CH(OH)CN + 2H_2O + HCl \longrightarrow CH_3CH(OH)COOH + NH_4Cl$

- be reduced by heating in hydrogen in the presence of a nickel catalyst to produce an amine group with an extra carbon in its chain, $-CH_2NH_2$

$$CH_3CH(OH)CN + 2H_2 \longrightarrow CH_3CH(OH)CH_2NH_2$$

You may be asked to predict the products or classify the types of reaction that occur on converting one compound into another. This scheme shows reactions involving carbonyl compounds:

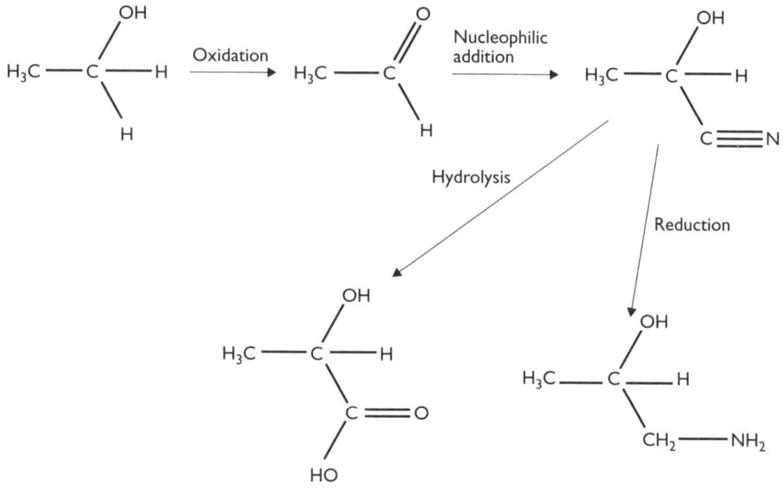

Carboxylic acids and esters

Carboxylic acids are weak acids but they will liberate CO_2 from carbonates and hydrogencarbonates. You need to be able to predict the structure of the different esters produced in esterification reactions. Esters have pleasant smells and are used in solvents, plasticisers and food flavourings. You need to be able to predict the products of ester hydrolysis.

It is important that you are familiar with a range of carboxylic acids because you should be able to predict their reactions with metals, alkalis, carbonates and alcohols.

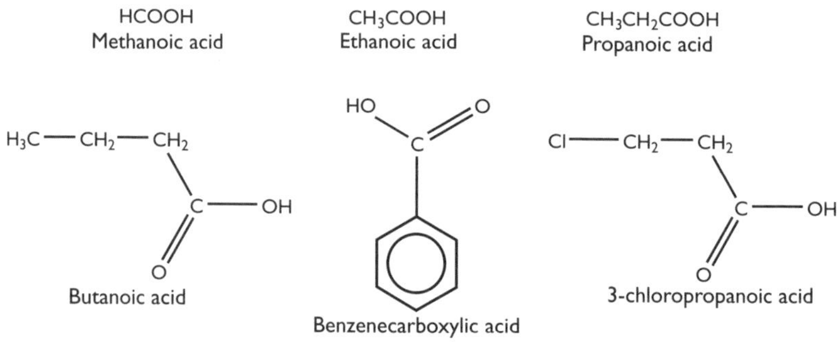

HCOOH
Methanoic acid

CH_3COOH
Ethanoic acid

CH_3CH_2COOH
Propanoic acid

Butanoic acid

Benzenecarboxylic acid

3-chloropropanoic acid

2-hydroxypropanoic acid (lactic acid)

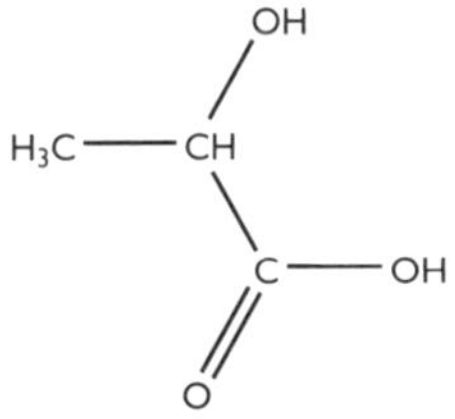

Ethanedioic acid (oxalic acid)

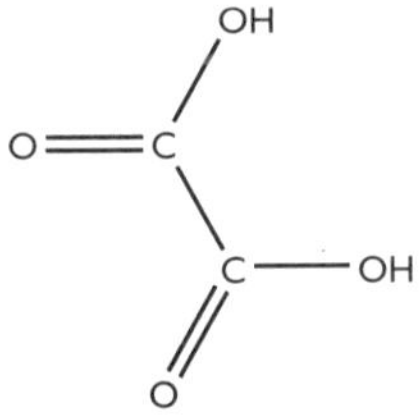

trans-butenedioic acid (fumaric acid)

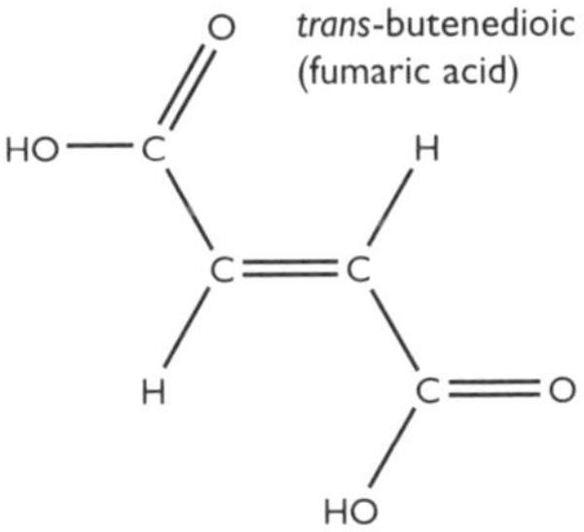

Chemical properties

Carboxylic acids are weak acids, which ionise partially in water to produce $H^+(aq)$ ions.

$$CH_3COOH(aq) \rightleftharpoons CH_3COO^-(aq) + H^+(aq)$$

Carboxylic acids vary in strength, depending on the groups attached to the –COOH group. The acid strength is shown by the K_a value. The higher the K_a value, the greater is the dissociation of the acid, and the greater the strength of the acid.

Carboxylic acids react as typical acids. Ethanoic acid is used as an example:

Type of reactant	Equation
Metals	$CH_3COOH + Na \longrightarrow CH_3COONa + \frac{1}{2}H_2$
Alkalis	$CH_3COOH + NaOH \longrightarrow CH_3COONa + H_2O$
Carbonates	$2CH_3COOH + Na_2CO_3 \longrightarrow 2CH_3COONa + H_2O + CO_2$
Hydrogencarbonates	$CH_3COOH + NaHCO_3 \longrightarrow CH_3COONa + H_2O + CO_2$

The reaction with Na_2CO_3 or $NaHCO_3$ is used to test for carboxylic acids. The production of CO_2 indicates the presence of the –COOH group.

Esters

Nomenclature

Look at the structures of a selection of esters and note how they are named according to the acid and alcohol from which they are made.

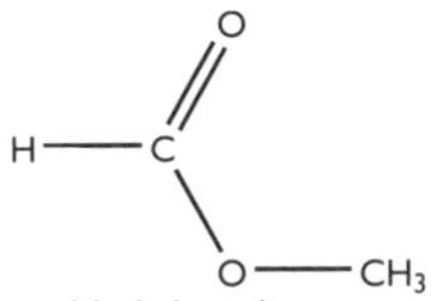

Methyl methanoate

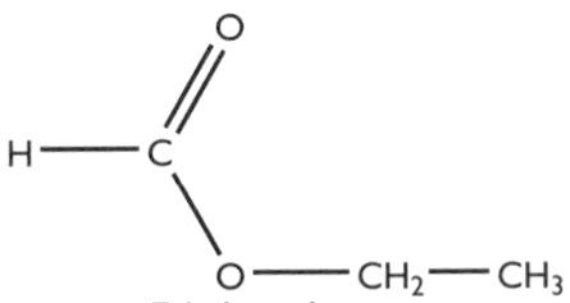

Ethyl methanoate

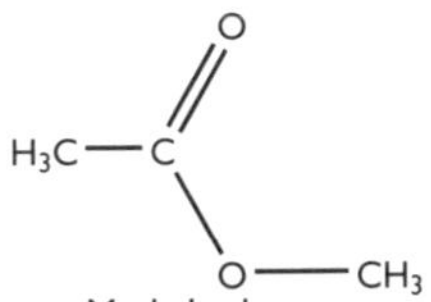

Methyl ethanoate

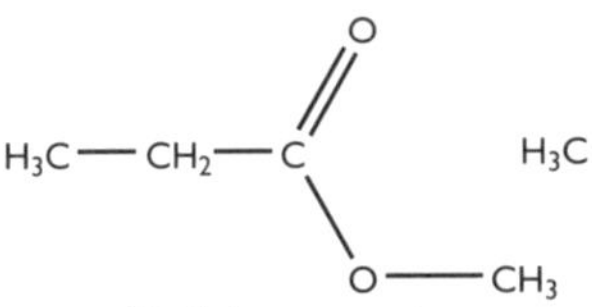

Methyl propanoate

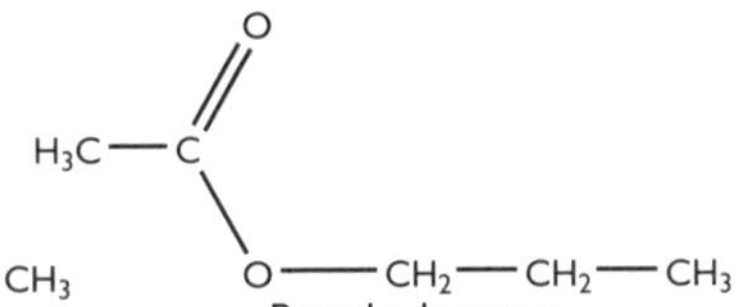

Propyl ethanoate

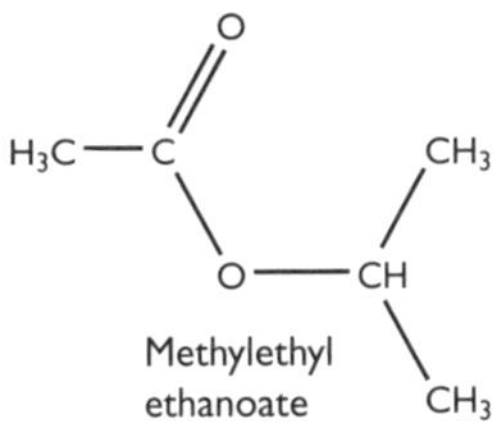

Methylethyl ethanoate

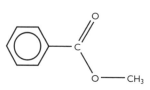

Methyl benzenecarboxylate   Phenyl ethanoate

Preparation

The reaction is:

acid + alcohol $\rightleftharpoons$ ester + water

$$R_1-\overset{\overset{O}{\|}}{\underset{\underset{OH}{|}}{C}} \quad + \quad H-OR_2 \quad \longrightarrow \quad R_1-\overset{\overset{O}{\|}}{\underset{\underset{OR_2}{|}}{C}} \quad + \quad H_2O$$

The carboxylic acid loses the OH
and the alcohol loses the H

The acid and alcohol mixture is warmed in the presence of a concentrated H_2SO_4 catalyst.

$$H_3C-OH \;+\; H_3C-\overset{\overset{O}{\|}}{\underset{\underset{OH}{|}}{C}} \;\rightleftharpoons\; H_3C-\overset{\overset{O}{\|}}{\underset{\underset{O-CH_3}{|}}{C}} \;+\; H_2O$$

Methanol   Ethanoic acid   Methyl ethanoate

You should be able to predict the acids and alcohols used to prepare esters. For example, ethyl methanoate is prepared from ethanol and methanoic acid.

Common uses

- **Solvents** — esters dissolve many polar organic compounds and are volatile, so they are easily separated from the solute. For example, ethyl ethanoate is used in nail varnish, polystyrene cement and printing inks.
- **Plasticisers** — these are added to plastics to improve flexibility, for example esters of benzene-1,2-dicarboxylic acid (phthalic acid) are added to PVC. However, over time, the additives escape and the plastics become brittle.
- **Food flavourings** — these often have sweet or fruity smells, for example pentyl ethanoate (pear) and octyl ethanoate (orange).
- **Perfumes** — when mixed with other compounds (such as alcohols). An example is pentyl 2-hydroxybenzenecarboxylate (jasmine).

Hydrolysis

The scheme below shows both the acidic and alkaline hydrolysis of esters.

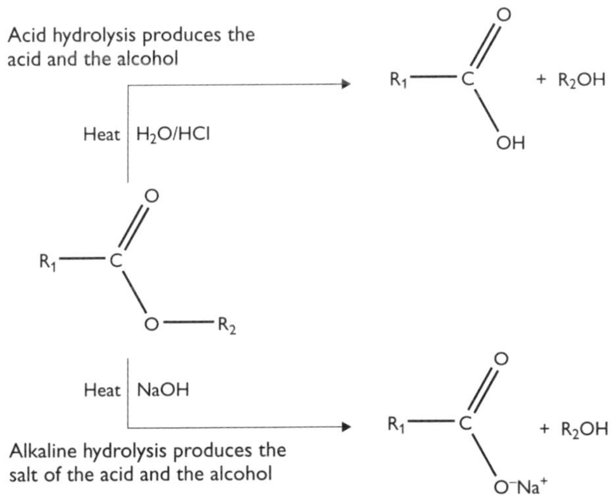

Acid hydrolysis produces the acid and the alcohol

Heat | H_2O/HCl

Heat | NaOH

Alkaline hydrolysis produces the salt of the acid and the alcohol

The acid hydrolysis of ethyl methanoate is represented by:

$$HCOOCH_2CH_3 + H_2O \longrightarrow HCOOH + CH_3CH_2OH$$

The alkaline hydrolysis of propyl ethanoate is represented by:

$$CH_3COOCH_2CH_2CH_3 + NaOH \longrightarrow CH_3COONa + CH_3CH_2CH_2OH$$

The alkaline hydrolysis of fats and oils

Fats and oils are esters of propane-1,2,3-triol (glycerol) and long-chain carboxylic acids called fatty acids. Examples of fatty acids include octadecanoic acid (stearic acid) and octadeca-9-enoic acid (oleic acid) The esters formed between glycerol and these fatty acids are called **triglycerides**. Triglycerides can be hydrolysed by NaOH.

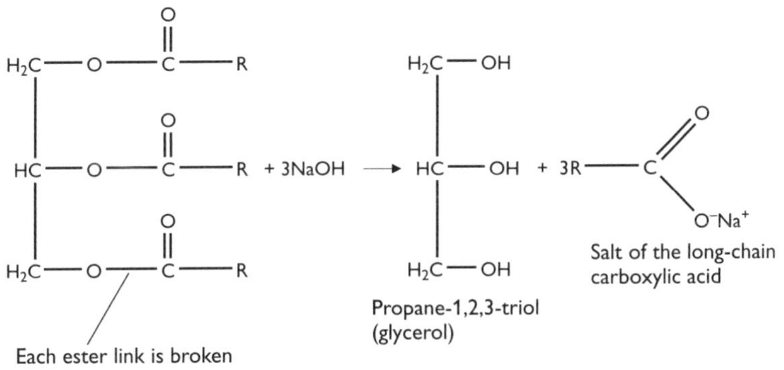

Each ester link is broken

Propane-1,2,3-triol (glycerol)

Salt of the long-chain carboxylic acid

If the acid is octadecanoic acid, then R = $-(CH_2)_{16}CH_3$ and the salt produced is sodium octadecanoate (sodium stearate), $CH_3(CH_2)_{16}COONa$, or simply soap.

Glycerol has three –OH groups and therefore exhibits extensive hydrogen bonding, so it has a high affinity for water. It is added to food and glues to prevent them drying out too quickly. It is also an important component of wine.

Acylation

The reagents used in acylation are acyl chlorides and acid anhydrides. You need to be able to write acylation equations using these reagents with water, alcohols, ammonia and amines, and understand the mechanisms for acylation involving acyl chlorides. You should be familiar with the manufacture of aspirin and the industrial advantages of ethanoic anhydride over ethanoyl chloride as the reagent for acylation.

Introduction

Acylation involves the introduction of an acyl group into an organic compound.

In acyl chlorides X = Cl. In acid anhydrides X = OCOR.

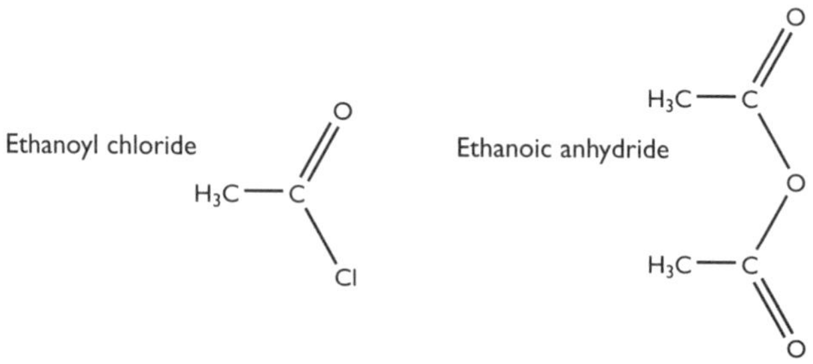

Both ethanoyl chloride and ethanoic anhydride are susceptible to nucleophilic attack. The groups (Cl or CH_3COO) attached to the carbon in the C=O bond are strongly electron withdrawing, so they make the carbon electron deficient. The Cl^- ion and the CH_3COO^- group are stable and so act as good leaving groups. Typical nucleophiles are water, alcohols, ammonia and amines.

Mechanism of nucleophilic addition–elimination

The general mechanism is shown below; H–Nu represents the nucleophile. The mechanisms for all four acylation reactions follow the same general pattern:

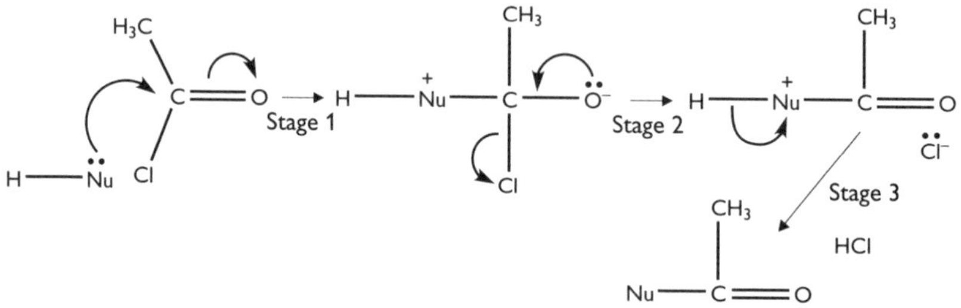

- Stage 1: the nucleophile attacks the C=O group to form an addition product; the C=O forms C–O⁻.

- Stage 2: Cl⁻ leaves and the C=O re-forms.
- Stage 3: H⁺ leaves and the final product is formed.

Example 1: with water to form ethanoic acid

Example 2: with ethanol to form ethyl ethanoate

Example 3: with ammonia to form ethanamide

Example 4: with phenylamine to form N-phenylethanamide

Equations

Once you understand the mechanism, the equations become easy to predict. Acyl chlorides and acid anhydrides show similar reactions, but acid anhydrides are less vigorous. However, acid anhydrides produce co-products, which are not easily removed from the reaction mixture.

Example 1: with water to produce carboxylic acids

$$CH_3COCl + H_2O \longrightarrow CH_3COOH + HCl$$
Ethanoic acid

$$(CH_3CO)_2O + H_2O \longrightarrow 2CH_3COOH$$

Example 2: with alcohols to produce esters

The reaction of acyl chlorides with alcohols is a more effective method of preparing esters than esterification; acylation is complete, whereas esterification is an equilibrium.

$$CH_3COCl + CH_3OH \longrightarrow CH_3COOCH_3 + HCl$$
Methyl ethanoate

$$(CH_3CO)_2O + CH_3OH \longrightarrow CH_3COOCH_3 + CH_3COOH$$

Example 3: with ammonia to produce amides

$$CH_3COCl + 2NH_3 \longrightarrow CH_3CONH_2 + NH_4^+Cl^-$$
Ethanamide

$$(CH_3CO)_2O + 2NH_3 \longrightarrow CH_3CONH_2 + CH_3COO^-NH_4^+$$
Ammonium
ethanoate

Example 4: with amines to produce N-substituted amides

$$CH_3COCl + 2CH_3NH_2 \longrightarrow CH_3CONHCH_3 + CH_3NH_3^+Cl^-$$
N-methylethanamide

$$(CH_3CO)_2O + 2CH_3NH_2 \longrightarrow CH_3CONHCH_3 + H_3C-\overset{\displaystyle O}{\underset{\displaystyle O^-}{C}} \quad H_3C-NH_3^+$$

$$CH_3COCl + 2 \underset{}{\text{(phenyl ring with } NH_2)} \longrightarrow H_3C-\overset{\displaystyle O}{C}\underset{\displaystyle NH-\text{(phenyl)}}{} + \underset{}{NH_3^+Cl^- \text{ (phenyl ring)}}$$

N-phenylethanamide

Aspirin

Aspirin is a drug that is used widely, often as an analgesic (pain-killer). There are two possible methods for its production. The –OH group in 2-hydroxybenzenecarboxylic acid undergoes acylation with either ethanoyl chloride or ethanoic anhydride.

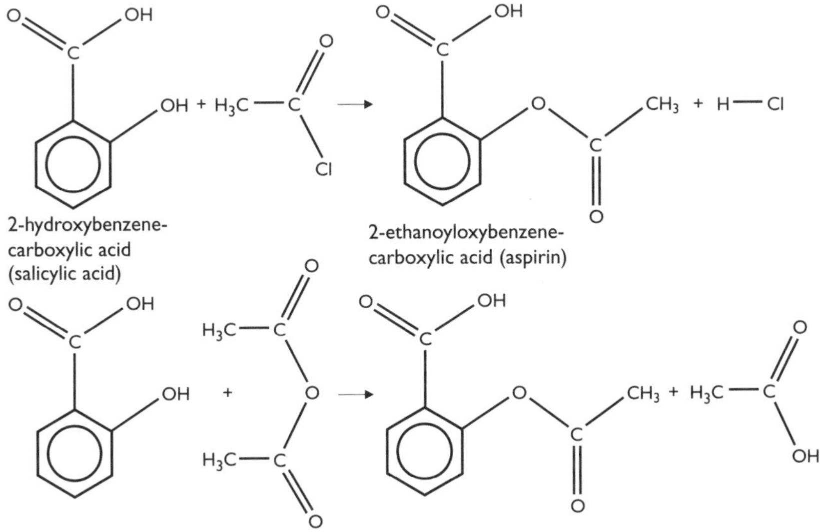

2-hydroxybenzene-
carboxylic acid
(salicylic acid)

2-ethanoyloxybenzene-
carboxylic acid (aspirin)

The production of aspirin on a large scale is achieved using ethanoic anhydride as the acylating agent. The main advantages of ethanoic anhydride are that it is:
- cheaper than ethanoyl chloride
- less corrosive
- less vulnerable to hydrolysis
- less dangerous to use

Aromatic chemistry

Benzene is a planar molecule with bond lengths intermediate between those of single and double bonds. You need to understand the unique nature of the bonding in the benzene ring, with its delocalised electrons, and that this delocalisation leads to increased stability in the benzene molecule.

The chemistry of aromatic compounds (arenes) is dominated by electrophilic substitution. You should learn the details of nitration, Friedel–Crafts alkylation and Friedel–Crafts acylation.

You need to be able to recall some facts about industrial chemistry involving arenes: the importance of nitration in the manufacture of explosives and the preparation of amines, from which dyes are made, and also the industrial-scale manufacture of ethyl-benzene and the use of ethylbenzene in the preparation of polystyrene.

The structure of benzene

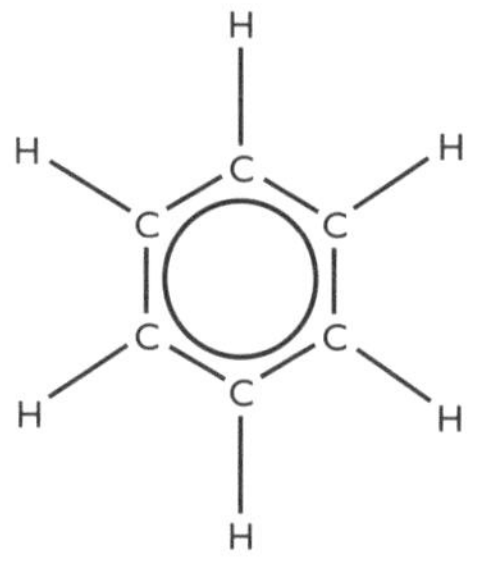

The key points are:
- It is a planar hexagonal molecule of six carbon atoms.
- Each carbon bears a hydrogen atom.
- All bond angles are equal at 120°.
- All carbon–carbon bond lengths are equal.
- All bond lengths are intermediate between a single C–C bond and a double C=C bond.
- The circle represents a ring of six delocalised electrons.

The stability of benzene

Benzene is more stable than expected owing to the presence of delocalised electrons. This can be shown by comparing the enthalpies of hydrogenation of cyclohexene, cyclohexa-1,3,5-triene and benzene.

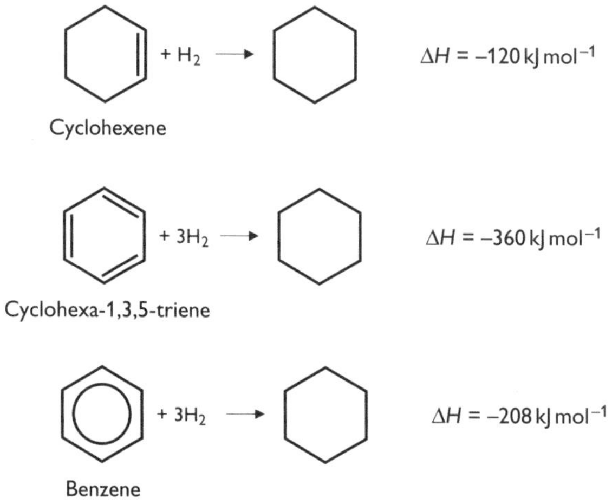

$+ H_2 \longrightarrow$ $\Delta H = -120\,kJ\,mol^{-1}$

Cyclohexene

$+ 3H_2 \longrightarrow$ $\Delta H = -360\,kJ\,mol^{-1}$

Cyclohexa-1,3,5-triene

$+ 3H_2 \longrightarrow$ $\Delta H = -208\,kJ\,mol^{-1}$

Benzene

This possible structure of alternate single and double bonds for benzene would be expected to release three times the $-120\,kJ\,mol^{-1}$ of cyclohexene because it contains three times as many double bonds.

The enthalpy of hydrogenation of benzene is only $-208\,kJ\,mol^{-1}$; this is $152\,kJ\,mol^{-1}$ less than expected. Benzene requires the extra $152\,kJ\,mol^{-1}$ of energy to break the bonds — it is more stable than expected because of the ring of delocalised electrons. This extra stability is called the **delocalisation energy**.

Electrophilic substitution

Benzene, with its ring of delocalised electrons, is electron rich. This means that benzene is susceptible to attack by electrophiles, which are electron-pair acceptors.

The initial attack by the electrophile creates a positive intermediate, similar to the carbocation in the reaction of alkenes with electrophiles. However, this intermediate loses a proton in the second stage of the mechanism and the ring of delocalised electrons re-forms. Benzene undergoes substitution rather than addition in order to retain the stability associated with the ring of delocalised electrons.

Nitration

- **Reagents:** concentrated nitric acid (HNO_3) and concentrated sulphuric acid (H_2SO_4)
- **Equation:** $C_6H_6 + HNO_3 \longrightarrow C_6H_5NO_2 + H_2O$
- **Formation of the electrophile:** the concentrated sulphuric acid acts as a strong acid and donates an H^+ ion to the nitric acid. This produces the nitronium ion, NO_2^+, which acts as an electrophile.

$$HNO_3 + H_2SO_4 \rightleftharpoons H_2NO_3^+ + HSO_4^-$$
$$H_2NO_3^+ \rightleftharpoons H_2O + NO_2^+$$
$$H_2SO_4 + H_2O \rightleftharpoons HSO_4^- + H_3O^+$$
Overall: $HNO_3 + 2H_2SO_4 \rightleftharpoons NO_2^+ + 2HSO_4^- + H_3O^+$

- **Mechanism:**

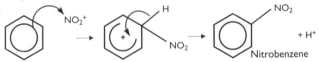

Importance of nitration
Polynitro compounds are unstable and decompose explosively to produce stable nitrogen, so they are used as explosives. The nitration of methylbenzene (toluene) produces a poly-substituted product because the $-CH_3$ group is electron releasing. This makes the ring more electron rich and more susceptible to electrophilic attack. 2,4,6-trinitrotoluene is better known as TNT.

Nitro compounds (containing $-NO_2$) can be easily reduced to amines (containing $-NH_2$). Amines can be converted to diazonium salts, which are used in the production of dyes.

Friedel–Crafts alkylation

- **Reagents:** a haloalkane (e.g. CH_3Cl) and aluminium chloride ($AlCl_3$)
- **Equation:** $C_6H_6 + CH_3Cl \longrightarrow C_6H_5CH_3 + HCl$
- **Formation of the electrophile:** the aluminium chloride acts as a Lewis acid catalyst (an electron-pair acceptor) and accepts an electron pair from the chlorine, forming $AlCl_4^-$ and the electrophile CH_3^+.

$$CH_3Cl + AlCl_3 \longrightarrow CH_3^+ + AlCl_4^-$$

- **Mechanism:**

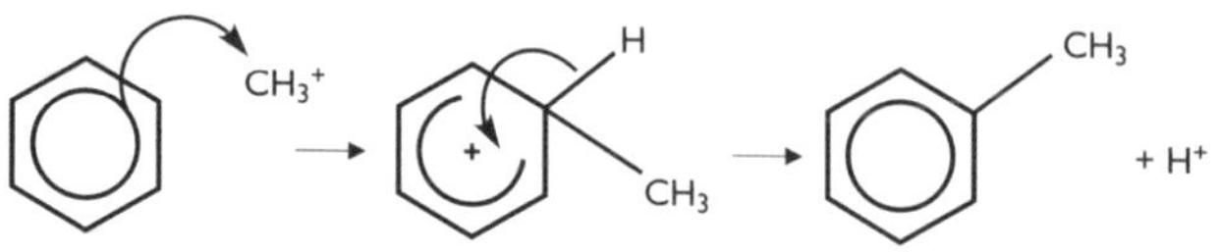

Alkyl groups are electron releasing, so the benzene ring becomes more electron rich. This makes it difficult to prevent further substitution and other alkyl groups will substitute into the benzene ring.

Friedel–Crafts acylation

- **Reagents:** an acyl chloride (e.g. CH_3COCl) and aluminium chloride ($AlCl_3$)
- **Equation:** $C_6H_6 + CH_3COCl \longrightarrow C_6H_5COCH_3 + HCl$
- **Formation of the electrophile:** the aluminium chloride acts as a Lewis acid catalyst and accepts an electron pair from the chlorine, forming $AlCl_4^-$ and the electrophile CH_3CO^+:

$$CH_3COCl + AlCl_3 \longrightarrow CH_3CO^+ + AlCl_4^-$$

- **Mechanism:**

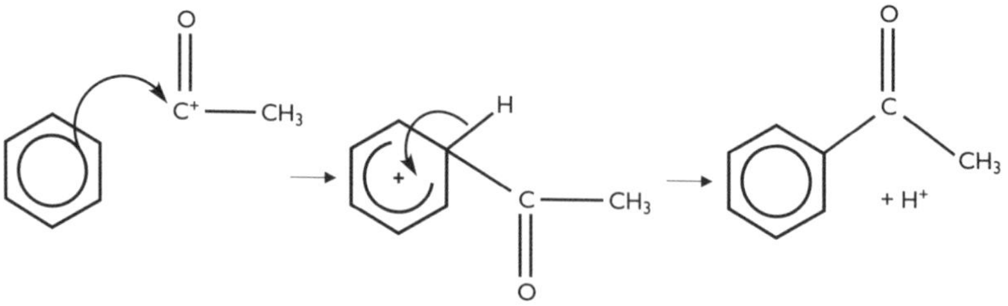

Advantages of acylation

In contrast to alkyl groups, the acyl group is electron withdrawing and this prevents further substitution, leading to a mono-substituted product. The acyl group can then be reduced with Zn/Hg and HCl to produce the alkyl side-chain.

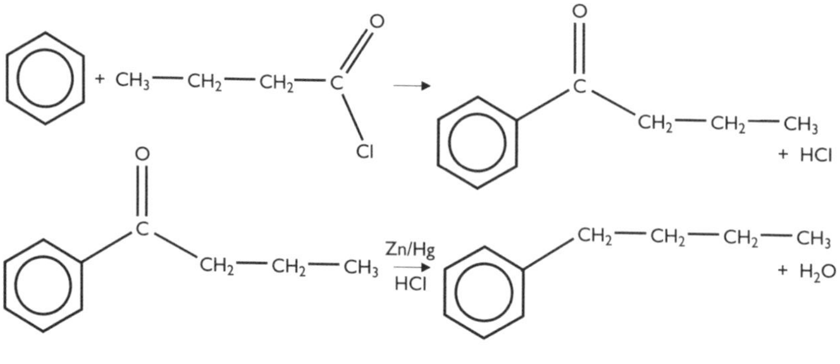

The industrial production of ethylbenzene

- **Reagents:** ethene ($CH_2=CH_2$), hydrogen chloride (HCl) and aluminium chloride ($AlCl_3$). (Ethene is used, rather than chloroethane, because it is more readily available and cheaper.)

- **Formation of the electrophile:**

$$CH_2{=}CH_2 + HCl \longrightarrow CH_3CH_2{}^+Cl^-$$
$$CH_3CH_2{}^+Cl^- + AlCl_3 \longrightarrow CH_3CH_2{}^+AlCl_4{}^-$$

- **Mechanism:**

Ethylbenzene

Polystyrene production

Ethylbenzene undergoes dehydrogenation when heated at 600°C in the presence of an iron oxide catalyst to produce phenylethene (formerly called styrene).

Phenylethene

Phenylethene undergoes addition polymerisation to produce poly(phenylethene), which is better known as polystyrene.

Amines

You need to understand the essential features of Brønsted–Lowry bases and Lewis bases and be able to use these to explain the differences in the base strength of ammonia, primary aliphatic amines (e.g. ethylamine) and primary aromatic amines (e.g. phenylamine) in terms of the availability of the lone pair on the nitrogen atom.

The chemistry of amines is dominated by their ability to act as nucleophiles due to the presence of the lone pair on the nitrogen atom. You need to be able to describe in detail (including the mechanisms) the nucleophilic substitution reactions of ammonia and amines with haloalkanes to form primary, secondary and tertiary amines and quaternary ammonium salts. You need to be able to recall the use of quaternary ammonium salts as cationic detergents.

Finally, you need to know the reagents and equations for the preparation of amines from haloalkanes and nitriles and the production of aromatic amines by the reduction of nitro compounds.

Basic properties

A Brønsted–Lowry base is defined as a proton acceptor. A Lewis base is defined as an electron-pair donor. Ammonia (NH_3) and amines (RNH_2) have a lone pair of electrons on the nitrogen, which can accept a proton. The reactions of ammonia with water and acid illustrate this.

$$NH_3 + H_2O \rightleftharpoons NH_4^+ + OH^-$$
$$NH_3 + HCl \rightleftharpoons NH_4^+ + Cl^-$$

The strength of a base can be expressed in terms of the constant K_b. For the reaction

$$RNH_2 + H_2O \rightleftharpoons RNH_3^+ + OH^-$$

$$K_b = \frac{[RNH_3^+][OH^-]}{[RNH_2]}$$

The larger the K_b value, the more protonation takes place and the stronger the base.

The strength of the base can also be expressed in terms of pK_b:

$$pK_b = -\log_{10} K_b$$

The larger the value of K_b the smaller is the value of pK_b, so the stronger the base.

The basic strength depends upon the availability of the lone pair. Compare ammonia, ethylamine and phenylamine:

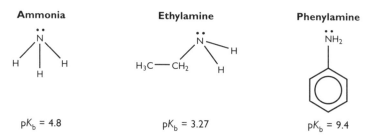

Ammonia	Ethylamine	Phenylamine
$pK_b = 4.8$	$pK_b = 3.27$	$pK_b = 9.4$

- Ammonia is used as the standard because it has no other groups attached.
- Ethylamine is a stronger base than ammonia because the lone pair on the nitrogen is more available due to the electron-releasing effect of the $-C_2H_5$ group.
- Phenylamine is a weaker base than ammonia because the lone pair is less available due to interaction with the delocalised electrons in the benzene ring.

Nucleophilic properties

A nucleophile is an electron-pair donor that attacks an electron-deficient site. Ammonia and amines have a lone pair on the nitrogen, so they act as nucleophiles and attack haloalkanes to give a mixture of products. For example:

$$CH_3CH_2Br + NH_3 \longrightarrow CH_3CH_2NH_3^+Br^-$$
$$CH_3CH_2NH_3^+Br^- + NH_3 \longrightarrow CH_3CH_2NH_2 + NH_4Br$$
$$\text{primary amine}$$

This is a nucleophilic substitution reaction and the initial product is ethylamine — a primary amine. If excess ammonia is used, the major product is ethylamine.

If excess bromoethane is used, further substitution reactions take place to produce a mixture of products — secondary and tertiary amines and quaternary ammonium salts.

Each amine can continue to attack the haloalkane because the amine still has a lone pair on the nitrogen atom. If a large excess of bromoethane is used, a high yield of the quaternary ammonium salt is produced.

$$CH_3CH_2Br + CH_3CH_2NH_2 \longrightarrow (CH_3CH_2)_2NH_2^+Br^-$$
$$(CH_3CH_2)_2NH_2^+Br^- + NH_3 \longrightarrow (CH_3CH_2)_2NH + NH_4Br$$
secondary amine

$$CH_3CH_2Br + (CH_3CH_2)_2NH \longrightarrow (CH_3CH_2)_3NH^+Br^-$$
$$(CH_3CH_2)_3NH^+Br^- + NH_3 \longrightarrow (CH_3CH_2)_3N + NH_4Br$$
tertiary amine

$$CH_3CH_2Br + (CH_3CH_2)_3N \longrightarrow (CH_3CH_2)_4N^+Br^-$$
quaternary ammonium salt

Quaternary ammonium salts are used in the production of cationic detergents, which are found in fabric softeners. The cationic detergent is added to the final rinse, after using anionic detergents, to impart a softer feel to the fabric. A typical cationic detergent contains two long-chain alkyl groups, for example $[CH_3(CH_2)_{17}]_2N(CH_3)_2^+Cl^-$.

The preparation of amines

Nucleophilic substitution of haloalkanes

- **Reagents:** haloalkane (e.g. bromoethane) and excess ammonia in ethanol
- **Equation:** $CH_3CH_2Br + 2NH_3 \longrightarrow CH_3CH_2NH_2 + NH_4^+Br^-$
- **Mechanism:**

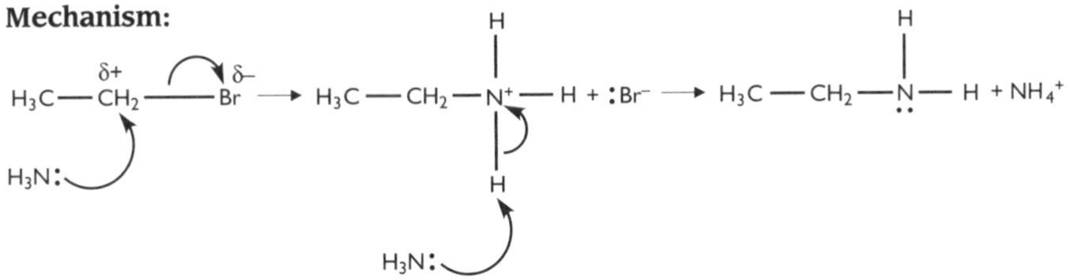

If the bromoethane is in excess, the ethylamine attacks the bromoethane again to produce diethylamine. The reaction will continue until the quaternary ammonium salt is produced.

The reduction of nitriles

- **Reagents:** nitrile (e.g. propanenitrile), hydrogen and a nickel catalyst *or* LiAlH$_4$ in dry ether
- **Equations:**
$$CH_3CH_2CN + 2H_2 \longrightarrow CH_3CH_2CH_2NH_2$$
$$CH_3CH_2CN + 4[H] \longrightarrow CH_3CH_2CH_2NH_2$$

This route has two major advantages over the preparation of amines from haloalkanes — it gives a much better yield and there are no other products.

Reduction of aromatic nitro compounds

- **Reagents:** nitrobenzene, hydrogen and a nickel catalyst *or* tin and concentrated HCl
- **Equations:**

$$C_6H_5NO_2 + 3H_2 \longrightarrow C_6H_5NH_2 + 2H_2O$$
$$C_6H_5NO_2 + 6[H] \longrightarrow C_6H_5NH_2 + 2H_2O$$

Amino acids

Amino acids have both acidic and basic properties due to the presence of the –COOH group and the –NH$_2$ group. They join together by peptide links to produce proteins, which can undergo hydrolysis at the peptide links to produce the constituent amino acids. You need to understand the importance of hydrogen bonding in proteins.

Structure

Amino acids contain a primary amino group (–NH$_2$) and a carboxyl group (–COOH). The primary amino group is attached to the carbon atom adjacent to the –COOH group, which is called the α-carbon. The molecules are referred to as α-amino carboxylic acids.

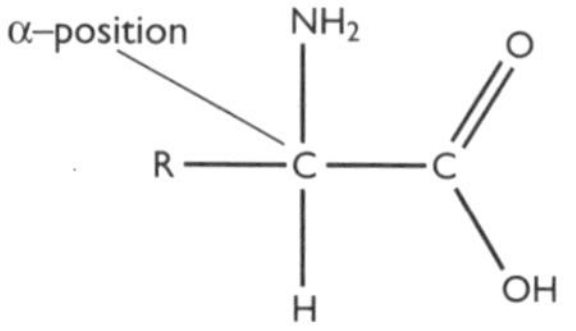

There are 20 naturally occurring amino acids, which differ in the nature of the R group (see the structure above).

- The simplest has R = H; this is aminoethanoic acid (glycine), which is not optically active.
- All the other amino acids are optically active because they have four different groups attached to the α-carbon.

Amino acids are called by their trivial names and abbreviations are often used.

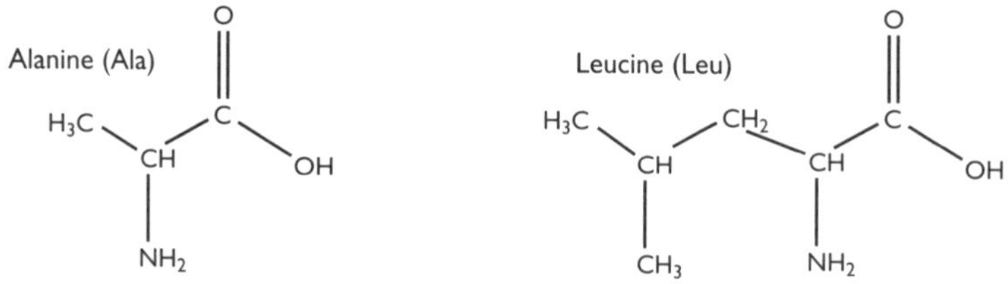

Acid and base properties

Acid and base properties are demonstrated by all amino acids. This is illustrated below using glycine as an example.

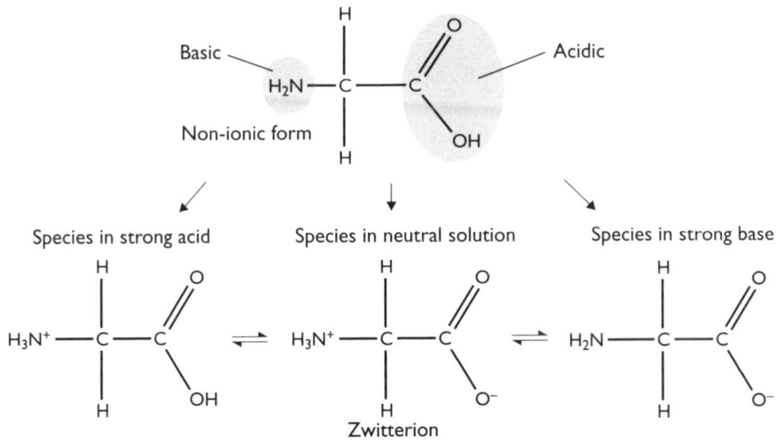

Isoelectric point

The isoelectric point (IEP) of an amino acid is the pH at which it has no net charge. It varies, depending on the R group. At the IEP, an amino acid exists as dipolar ions, $RCH(NH_3^+)COO^-$, called **zwitterions**, as shown above.

The ionic nature of amino acids explains why they have such high melting points (e.g. glycine, 290°C).

Proteins

Amino acids link together to form polymers (called polypeptides and proteins). They link together through the formation of an amide group (–CONH), which is called a **peptide link**.

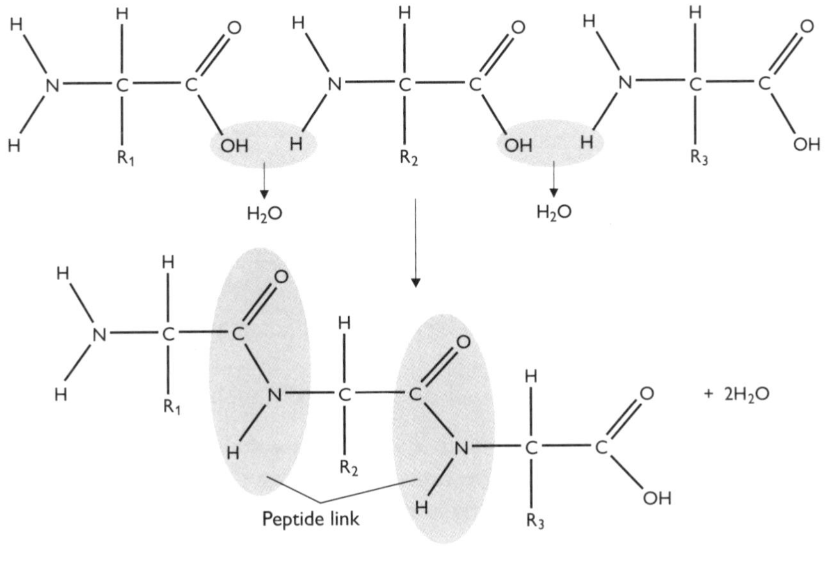

The polymers show a range of relative molecular masses, for example:
- insulin, $M_r = 5700$, contains 51 amino acid residues
- haemoglobin, $M_r = 66\,000$, contains 574 amino acid residues

Hydrolysis of proteins

Proteins and polypeptides can be hydrolysed into their constituent amino acids. Hydrolysis is caused by reaction with an acid or a specific enzyme.

The C–N bond in the amide group splits

Hydrogen bonding in proteins

- The primary structure of a protein is the sequence of amino acids.
- The secondary structure of a protein is governed by hydrogen bonding, which results in the formation of helices or sheets. The hydrogen bonds occur between the atoms of the peptide links. A large number of hydrogen bonds increases the forces between the polymers and forms stable structures.

Polymers

Addition polymers are formed from alkenes. Polyalkenes are saturated, non-polar molecules that are chemically inert and are therefore non-biodegradable. You need to be able to predict the polymer structure from a given monomer and vice versa.

You need to understand the three methods of forming condensation polymers and know how the repeating units of polyesters and polyamides are linked. Polyesters and polyamides can be broken down by hydrolysis and are therefore biodegradable.

Addition polymers

Addition polymers are formed directly from compounds containing C=C bonds. The unsaturated molecules that add together are called **monomers**. The long chain of monomers linked together is called a **polymer**. The addition polymerisation process can be represented by:

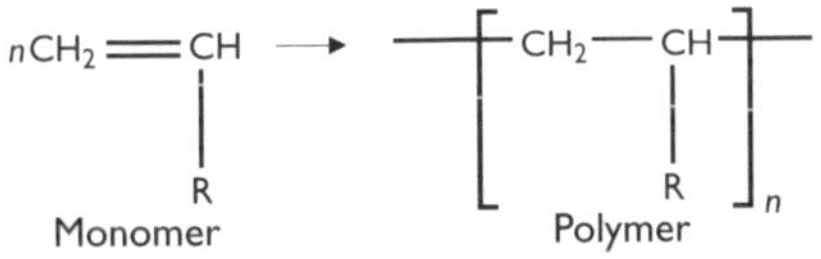

R represents groups such as H, CH_3, C_6H_5, Cl, CN or $OCOCH_3$. The repeating unit in the polymer is enclosed in square brackets and n is a number between 100 and 10 000.

The polymers are named as polyalkenes, but they are saturated molecules with C–C single bonds. They have no bond polarity so they are chemically inert and non-biodegradable. However, they are flammable and can burn to produce toxic products.

Example 1: ethene to poly(ethene) or polythene

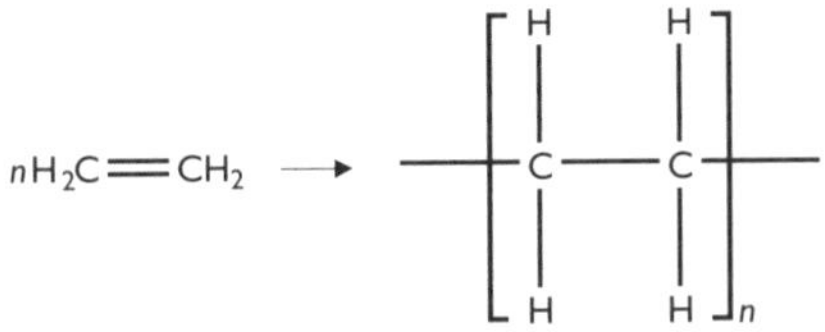

Example 2: phenylethene to poly(phenylethene) or polystyrene

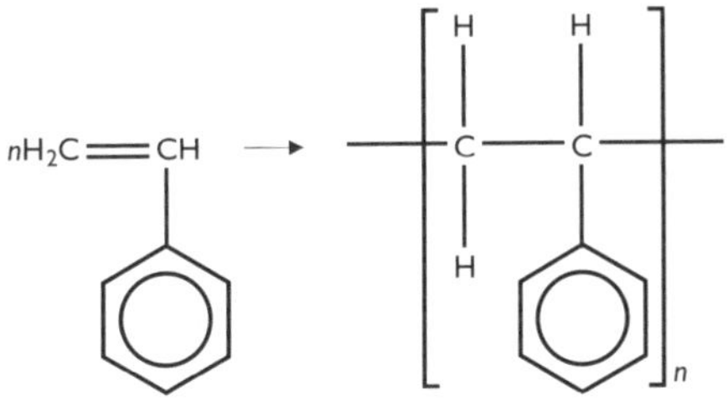

Condensation polymers

Formation

Condensation polymers are formed by the reaction between molecules with two functional groups and involve the loss of small molecules such as H_2O, HCl or CH_3OH.
- The reaction between a dicarboxylic acid and a diamine leads to the formation of a polyamide.
- Amino acids can also be polymerised to form polyamides.
- The reaction between a dicarboxylic acid and a diol leads to the formation of a polyester.

Example 1: the formation of nylon-6,6, a polyamide

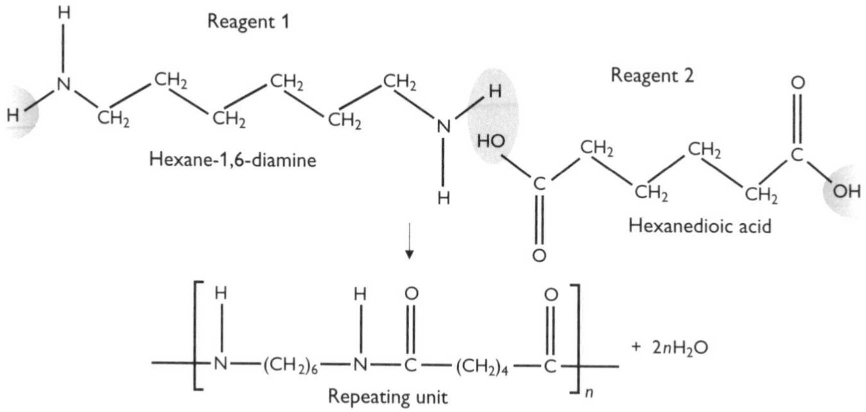

Hexane-1,6-diamine

Reagent 1

Reagent 2

Hexanedioic acid

Repeating unit

$+ 2nH_2O$

Example 2: the formation of nylon-6, a polyamide

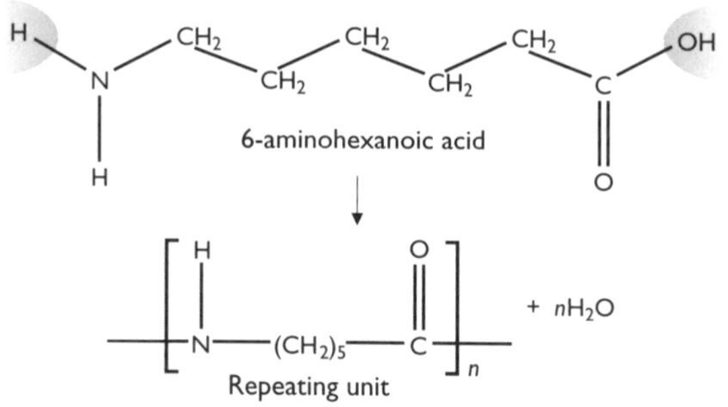

6-aminohexanoic acid

Repeating unit

$+ nH_2O$

Example 3: the formation of terylene, a polyester

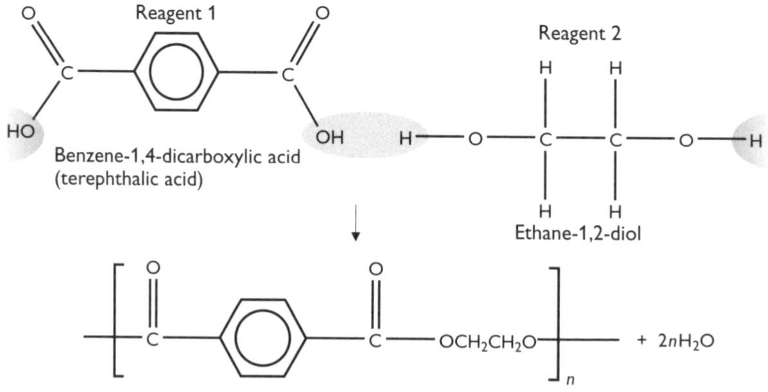

Reagent 1

Reagent 2

Benzene-1,4-dicarboxylic acid
(terephthalic acid)

Ethane-1,2-diol

$+ 2nH_2O$

Hydrolysis

When polyamides or polyesters are warmed with sodium hydroxide or hydrochloric acid they undergo hydrolysis. The polymer chains are broken down into their component monomers, which means they are biodegradable.

Organic synthesis and analysis

You need to be able to use the organic reactions covered in this module to convert one functional group to another in a multi-step process. You need to be able to identify the functional groups covered in this module and in AS Module 3 (alkenes, haloalkanes and alcohols) by their characteristic reactions.

You will be expected to look at a multi-step process. For each individual step, you could be asked to:
- state the **reagents** used in the conversion
- classify the **reaction type**
- name and outline the **mechanism**
- draw and name the structures of the **intermediates**
- predict the final **product**

Synthesis

Reactions

The tables below summarise the conversion of one functional group to another.

Reactions of alkenes

Conversion	Formulae	Reagents and conditions	Reaction type/ mechanism
Alkene → haloalkane	$RCH=CH_2$ → $RCHBrCH_3$	HBr	Electrophilic addition
Alkene → dihaloalkane	$RCH=CH_2$ → $RCHBrCH_2Br$	Br_2 in an organic solvent	Electrophilic addition
Alkene → alcohol	$RCH=CH_2$ → $RCH(OH)CH_3$	Concentrated H_2SO_4 followed by H_2O	Electrophilic addition followed by hydrolysis

Reactions of haloalkanes

Conversion	Formulae	Reagents and conditions	Reaction type/ mechanism
Haloalkane → nitrile	RBr → RCN	NaCN in ethanol and reflux	Nucleophilic substitution
Haloalkane → alcohol	RBr → ROH	NaOH in aqueous solvent and reflux	Nucleophilic substitution (hydrolysis)
Haloalkane → amine	RBr → RNH2	NH_3 in ethanol in a sealed vessel	Nucleophilic substitution
Haloalkane → alkene	RCH_2CH_2Br → $RCH=CH_2$	NaOH in alcoholic solvent and reflux	Elimination

Reactions of alcohols

Conversion	Formulae	Reagents and conditions	Reaction type/ mechanism
Primary alcohol → aldehyde	RCH_2OH → $RCHO$	Acidified $K_2Cr_2O_7$, *distillation*	Oxidation
Primary alcohol → acid	RCH_2OH → $RCOOH$	Acidified $K_2Cr_2O_7$, *reflux*	Oxidation
Secondary alcohol → ketone	R_1R_2CHOH → R_1R_2CO	Acidified $K_2Cr_2O_7$	Oxidation
Alcohol → alkene	RCH_2CH_2OH → $RCH=CH_2$	Concentrated H_2SO_4, heat	Elimination (dehydration)
Alcohol → ester	R_1OH → R_2COOR_1	Carboxylic acid (R_2COOH), concentrated H_2SO_4 as catalyst, warm	Esterification

Reactions of carbonyl groups

Conversion	Formulae	Reagents and conditions	Reaction type/ mechanism
Aldehyde → acid	$RCHO$ → $RCOOH$	Acidified $K_2Cr_2O_7$, reflux	Oxidation
Aldehyde → primary alcohol	$RCHO$ → RCH_2OH	Aqueous $NaBH_4$	Reduction
Ketone → secondary alcohol	R_2CO → R_2CHOH	Aqueous $NaBH_4$	Reduction
Aldehyde or ketone → hydroxynitrile	$RCHO$ → $RCH(OH)CN$	HCN	Nucleophilic addition

Reactions of nitriles

Conversion	Formulae	Reagents and conditions	Reaction type/ mechanism
Nitrile → carboxylic acid	RCN → $RCOOH$	Dilute acid (HCl), reflux	Hydrolysis
Nitrile → amine	RCN → RCH_2NH_2	H_2, Ni catalyst, heat or $LiAlH_4$ in dry ether	Reduction

Reactions of esters

Conversion	Formulae	Reagents and conditions	Reaction type/ mechanism
Ester → salt of acid + alcohol	R_1COOR_2 → $R_1COONa + R_2OH$	NaOH, reflux	Alkaline hydrolysis
Ester → acid + alcohol	R_1COOR_2 → $R_1COOH + R_2OH$	HCl, reflux	Acid hydrolysis

Reactions of acyl chlorides

Conversion	Formulae	Reagents and conditions	Reaction type/mechanism
Acyl chloride → acid	$RCOCl →$ $RCOOH$	H_2O	Nucleophilic addition–elimination (acylation)
Acyl chloride → ester	$R_1COCl →$ R_1COOR_2	Alcohol (R_2OH)	Nucleophilic addition–elimination (acylation)
Acyl chloride → amide	$RCOCl →$ $RCONH_2$	NH_3	Nucleophilic addition–elimination (acylation)
Acyl chloride → N-substituted amide	$R_1COCl →$ R_1CONHR_2	Amine (R_2NH_2)	Nucleophilic addition–elimination (acylation)

Reactions of aromatic compounds

Conversion	Formulae	Reagents and conditions	Reaction type/mechanism
Benzene → nitrobenzene	$C_6H_6 →$ $C_6H_5NO_2$	Concentrated HNO_3 and concentrated H_2SO_4, reflux	Electrophilic substitution (nitration)
Nitrobenzene → phenylamine	$C_6H_5NO_2 →$ $C_6H_5NH_2$	Tin, concentrated HCl, reflux	Reduction
Benzene → methylbenzene	$C_6H_6 →$ $C_6H_5CH_3$	CH_3Cl and $AlCl_3$	Electrophilic substitution (Friedel–Crafts alkylation)
Benzene → phenylethanone	$C_6H_6 →$ $C_6H_5COCH_3$	CH_3COCl and $AlCl_3$	Electrophilic substitution (Friedel–Crafts acylation)

Worked examples

It is essential that you learn *all* the reagents, conditions, types of reactions and mechanisms outlined in the tables above.

You may also be asked to write balanced equations for the conversions, to identify the names and structures of the intermediates or to outline a mechanism.

Example 1
Consider this reaction sequence.

(1) Name compounds A to E. (5 marks)

(2) Classify the reaction types for steps 2, 3 and 4. (3 marks)

(3) State the reagents and conditions needed for steps 2 and 4. (2 marks)

Answers

(1) A = propan-1-ol; B = 1-bromopropane; C = butanenitrile; D = butanoic acid; E = methyl butanoate

(2) Step 2 = nucleophilic substitution; step 3 = hydrolysis; step 4 = esterification

(3) Step 2 = NaCN in ethanol and reflux; step 4 = methanol, concentrated H_2SO_4 as catalyst, warm

Example 2

This reaction sequence shows the synthesis of 2-oxopropanoic acid.

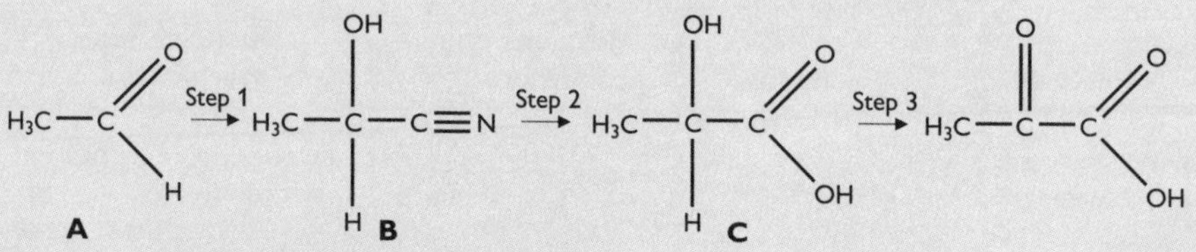

(1) Name compounds A, B and C. (3 marks)

(2) State the name of the mechanism in step 1. (1 mark)

(3) Classify the reaction types in steps 2 and 3. (2 marks)

(4) State the reagents required in steps 1, 2 and 3. (4 marks)

Answers

(1) A = ethanal; B = 2-hydroxypropanenitrile; C = 2-hydroxypropanoic acid

(2) Nucleophilic addition

(3) Step 2 = hydrolysis; step 3 = oxidation

(4) Step 1 = HCN; step 2 = dilute HCl; step 3 = dilute H_2SO_4 and $K_2Cr_2O_7$

Example 3

This reaction sequence shows the preparation of N-phenylethanamide from benzene.

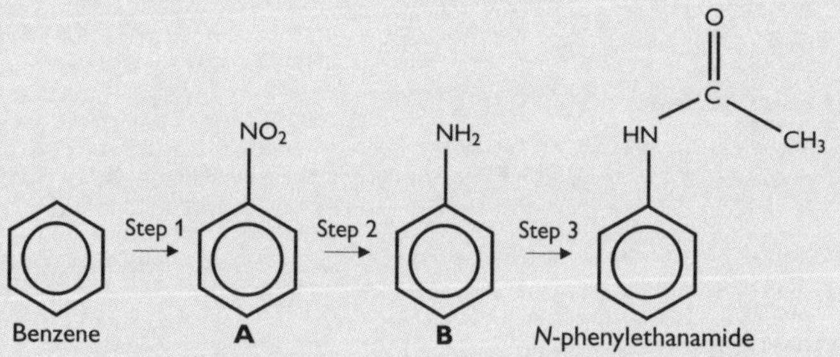

(1) Name the intermediates A and B. (2 marks)

(2) State the reagents used in step 1. (2 marks)

(3) State the name of the mechanism for step 1.   (1 mark)
(4) State the type of reaction in step 2.   (1 mark)
(5) State the reagents and conditions for step 2.   (3 marks)
(6) State the name of the mechanism for step 3.   (1 mark)

Answers
(1) A = nitrobenzene; B = phenylamine
(2) Concentrated nitric acid and concentrated sulphuric acid
(3) Electrophilic substitution
(4) Reduction
(5) Tin and concentrated hydrochloric acid; reflux
(6) Nucleophilic addition–elimination

Analysis

You need to be able to describe simple chemical tests that will distinguish between organic compounds containing different functional groups.

Alkenes
- **Test:** bromine water
  Observation: decolorises

Haloalkanes
- **Test:** warm with NaOH, acidify with HNO_3, then add $AgNO_3$
  Observation: chloroalkane gives a white precipitate of AgCl, bromoalkane gives a cream precipitate of AgBr and iodoalkane gives a yellow precipitate of AgI

Alcohols
- **Test:** acidified $K_2Cr_2O_7$
  Observation: primary and secondary alcohols turn the potassium dichromate solution from orange to green; tertiary alcohols give no colour change

- **Test:** warm with CH_3COOH in the presence of concentrated H_2SO_4
  Observation: smell of an ester

Aldehydes
- **Test:** acidified $K_2Cr_2O_7$
  Observation: potassium dichromate solution changes from orange to green

- **Test:** warm with Fehling's solution
  Observation: the Fehling's solution changes from a blue solution to a red precipitate of copper(I) oxide, Cu_2O

- **Test:** warm with Tollens' reagent
  Observation: the colourless solution forms a silver mirror

Carboxylic acids
- **Test:** warm with CH_3CH_2OH in the presence of concentrated sulphuric acid
  Observation: smell of an ester

- **Test:** add aqueous $NaHCO_3$ solution
  Observation: fizzing due to evolution of carbon dioxide gas (CO_2)

Acyl chlorides
- **Test:** add aqueous $AgNO_3$ solution
  Observation: a vigorous reaction takes place to liberate HCl; the HCl immediately reacts with the $AgNO_3$ to produce a white precipitate

Structure determination

Mass spectrometry

You need to be able to determine the molecular formula of a compound from the mass of the molecular ion, and understand the fragmentation of molecular ions to explain the appearance of the relative abundance spectrum. You should know that more stable species, such as carbocations and acylium ions, give higher peaks.

Molecular ion peaks

When the spectrum of an organic molecule is analysed, the peak with the highest mass:charge (m/z) ratio, known as the molecular ion or parent ion, corresponds to the relative molecular mass of the molecule. Many organic molecules appear to have the same molecular mass; for example, C_6H_{12} and C_5H_8O both have $M_r = 84$. However, if more accurate relative atomic masses are used, slightly different M_r values are obtained, for example $C_6H_{12} = 84.093895$ and $C_5H_8O = 84.057511$. High-resolution mass spectrometers are capable of measuring the precise m/z value of any molecular ion. From this, the formula of the molecular ion can be found.

The presence of chlorine or bromine in a molecule can often be detected by the ratio of the molecular ion peaks. For chlorine this is due to the difference in abundance of the two chlorine isotopes (75% ^{35}Cl and 25% ^{37}Cl, i.e. a 3:1 ratio of ^{35}Cl:^{37}Cl) and for bromine this is due to an equal abundance of the two isotopes ^{79}Br and ^{81}Br (a 1:1 ratio of ^{79}Br:^{81}Br):
- In monochloroalkanes, the ratio of the M to $M+2$ peaks is 3:1 — for example, CH_3Cl can exist as $CH_3{}^{35}Cl$ and $CH_3{}^{37}Cl$ in a 3:1 ratio, 2 mass units different.
- In dichloroalkanes, the ratio of the M to $M+2$ to $M+4$ peaks is 9:6:1 — for example, CH_2Cl_2 can exist as $CH_2{}^{35}Cl^{35}Cl$, $CH_2{}^{35}Cl^{37}Cl$ and $CH_2{}^{37}Cl^{37}Cl$ in a 9:6:1 ratio.
- In monobromoalkanes, the ratio of the M to $M+2$ peaks is 1:1 — for example, CH_3Br can exist as $CH_3{}^{79}Br$ and $CH_3{}^{81}Br$ in a 1:1 ratio.
- in dibromoalkanes, the ratio of the M to $M+2$ to $M+4$ peaks is 1:2:1.

An $M+1$ peak is due to the presence of the carbon-13 isotope. The ratio of the M to $M+1$ peak indicates how many carbon atoms are present in the molecule: one carbon-13 atom is present for every 1.1% in the $M+1$ peak. For example, the $M+1$ peak in propanone, at an m/z ratio of 59, is 3.3% the height of the M peak, at 58; this confirms that propanone contains three carbon atoms.

Fragmentation

Fragmentation of the molecular ion takes place to produce a characteristic pattern or stick diagram. The molecular ion has an unpaired electron, so it is a **radical cation**. When this molecular ion fragments, it produces a cation (which is detected) and a radical (which is undetected). The general equation for this fragmentation is as follows:

$$M^{+\bullet} \longrightarrow X^+ + Y^{\bullet}$$

The most common ion gives rise to the **base peak**. By convention, the base peak is given a relative abundance of 100%, and all other peaks are expressed as a percentage of this.

Molecular ions fragment where bonds are weakest and dominant peaks are associated with stable cations such as carbocations (CH_3^+, $C_2H_5^+$) and acylium cations (CH_3CO^+, $C_2H_5CO^+$).

The mass spectrum of butanone

The mass spectrum of butanone is used to illustrate these principles.

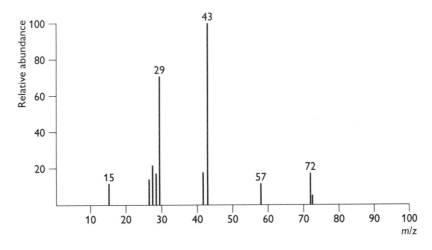

Butanone has the molecular formula C_4H_8O, so the molecular peak occurs at 72. The base peak is the most common peak and occurs at 43. Butanone has the structure shown. The arrows represent the bonds that break to produce the fragments at 15, 29, 43 and 57.

The four peaks are due to CH_3^+ at 15, $CH_3CH_2^+$ at 29, CH_3CO^+ at 43 and $CH_3CH_2CO^+$ at 57. The four fragments are formed from the parent ion as follows:

$$[CH_3COCH_2CH_3]^{+\bullet} \longrightarrow CH_3^+ + CH_3CH_2CO\bullet$$
$$[CH_3COCH_2CH_3]^{+\bullet} \longrightarrow CH_3CH_2^+ + CH_3CO\bullet$$
$$[CH_3COCH_2CH_3]^{+\bullet} \longrightarrow CH_3CO^+ + CH_3CH_2\bullet$$
$$[CH_3COCH_2CH_3]^{+\bullet} \longrightarrow CH_3CH_2CO^+ + CH_3\bullet$$

Infrared spectroscopy

You need to understand that functional groups absorb at characteristic frequencies. The fingerprint region is unique and is used to identify molecules by comparison with known spectra. You need to be able to identify functional groups and impurities in samples.

Basic principles

Bonds in molecules are not rigid; the atoms are free to stretch and bend. When infrared (IR) light is shone onto the molecules they stretch and bend more. The absorption of IR light occurs at particular wavenumbers, ranging from $400\,cm^{-1}$ to $4000\,cm^{-1}$. (Wavenumber is measured in cm^{-1} because it is $1/wavelength$.)

The position of the absorption depends on the bond strength and on the masses of the atoms involved. Strong bonds and light atoms absorb at high wavenumbers; weak bonds and heavy atoms absorb at low wavenumbers. Bending involves less energy than stretching, so bending absorptions occur at lower wavenumbers.

Functional groups in organic molecules give rise to characteristic absorptions, so IR spectra are useful in identifying them.

A typical simplified IR spectrum is shown below. It is split into four main regions and shows where the different functional groups absorb.

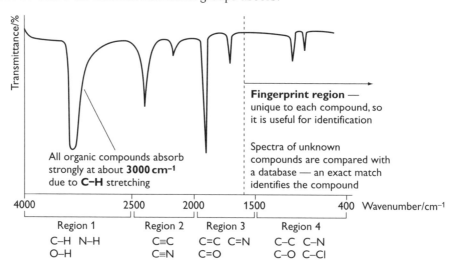

The most useful absorptions are:
- a broad O–H absorption between 2500 and 3500 cm^{-1}, which indicates a carboxylic acid
- a broad O–H absorption between 3000 and 3500 cm^{-1}, which indicates an alcohol
- a sharp, intense C=O absorption between 1680 and 1750 cm^{-1}, which could be due to an acid, ester or carbonyl

Applications

IR spectra are useful for identifying functional groups, especially when used with evidence from other spectra. They can be used to identify molecules because the 'fingerprint region' is unique to each molecule. If extra peaks are present in the spectra, these can be used to confirm the presence of impurities.

You may be asked to distinguish between different organic molecules. For example, if you were provided with an alcohol, an aldehyde and a carboxylic acid then it would be relatively easy to distinguish between the molecules using IR spectroscopy:
- The alcohol has a broad absorption due to the O–H group but not the sharp absorption of a C=O group.
- The aldehyde has no broad absorption because it does not have an O–H group. It has a sharp absorption due to the C=O group.
- The carboxylic acid has both a broad absorption due to the O–H group (at a slightly different value from the alcohol) and a sharp absorption due to the C=O group.

The simplified spectra are shown below.

The alcohol

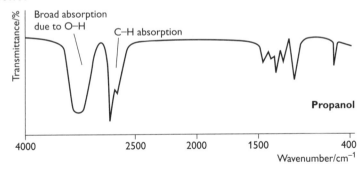

The aldehyde

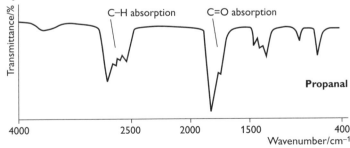

The carboxylic acid

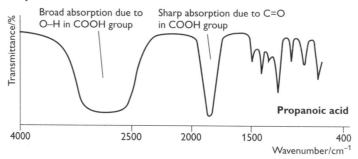

Nuclear magnetic resonance spectroscopy

You need to be able to use NMR spectra to deduce the relative number and position of hydrogen atoms in a molecule and to be able to describe the use of proton-free solvents in NMR spectra. You need to understand the use of tetramethylsilane (TMS) as the standard, the use of the chemical shift (δ) scale and how integrated spectra show the relative numbers of protons in different environments. Finally, you should be able to explain spin–spin splitting patterns of adjacent non-equivalent protons and to use the $n + 1$ rule.

Basic principles

Nuclear magnetic resonance (NMR) occurs in atoms with odd-numbered nuclei, such as ^1H and ^{13}C.

The nuclei of atoms such as ^1H have **nuclear spin** and possess a **magnetic moment**. This means that the nuclei behave like tiny bar magnets. When an external magnetic field is applied, the nucleus can have two spin states. It can either align itself with the external field (low-energy state) or against the field (high-energy state). A signal is recorded when a nucleus absorbs radiation in the radio-frequency range and resonates between the two spin states. Each nucleus in a unique environment within a molecule resonates at a specific frequency, resulting in characteristic peaks in the NMR spectrum.

The chemical environment

This discussion will now only look at ^1H spectra. ^1H nuclei are protons.

The protons in an organic molecule are surrounded by electrons in the molecule's covalent bonds. These electrons affect the NMR absorptions. The electrons are charged and have spin, so have their own magnetic field, which can shield the proton from the external field. The amount of shielding depends upon the electron density surrounding the nucleus, which varies for different protons within a molecule.

- The nucleus is **deshielded** when the electron density is reduced, owing to the presence of an electron-withdrawing group.

- The nucleus is **shielded** when the electron density is increased, owing to the presence of an electron-donating group.

Protons in different chemical environments give different peaks and chemically equivalent protons absorb at the same frequency. The movement of the signals caused by shielding (moving the signal upfield) and deshielding (moving the signal downfield) are measured by the chemical shift, δ. Chemical shifts are measured in parts per million (ppm) relative to an internal standard, **TMS**.

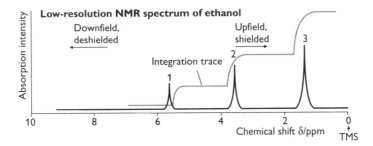

The internal standard

TMS is added to a sample being analysed to act as an internal standard:
- It gives a signal that resonates upfield from almost all other organic hydrogen resonances because the 12 equivalent hydrogens are highly shielded.
- It gives a single intense peak because there are 12 equivalent protons.
- It is non-toxic and inert.
- It has a low boiling point and can be easily removed from the sample being analysed.
- By definition, the δ value of TMS is zero and almost all proton NMR absorptions occur 0–10 ppm downfield from TMS.

The use of solvents
The sample being analysed must be dissolved in a solvent that is proton-free to avoid any unwanted absorptions. Typical solvents are CCl_4 and deuterated compounds such as $CDCl_3$ and C_6D_6, where $D = {}^2H$.

Low-resolution spectra

The *number* of absorptions indicates the number of non-equivalent protons that are present. For example, ethanol has three non-equivalent protons.

The *intensities* of the absorptions reveal how many protons are associated with that peak. In ethanol the absorptions are in the ratio 1:2:3, which are the –OH, the –CH$_2$– and –CH$_3$ groups. The relative intensities of the various absorptions can be measured electronically to provide an integration trace. The height of each step in the trace is proportional to the number of equivalent hydrogen atoms.

The *position* of the peaks gives information about the chemical environment of the proton. In ethanol, the closer the protons are to the electron-withdrawing oxygen atom the more deshielded they are and the further downfield they appear.

High-resolution spectra

The high-resolution spectrum of ethanol reveals that not all the absorptions are single peaks. The split peaks are shown as lines to simplify the diagram.

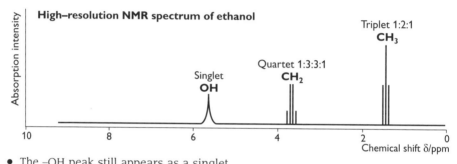

- The –OH peak still appears as a singlet.
- The –CH$_2$– group appears as a quartet, that is, the signal is split into four peaks.
- The –CH$_3$ group appears as a triplet, that is, the signal is split into three peaks.

Non-equivalent hydrogen atoms on adjacent carbon atoms interact or **couple** with the protons, causing this splitting of peaks. This is called **spin–spin coupling**. The splitting of an absorption signal is described by the $n + 1$ rule. Signals for protons adjacent to n equivalent neighbours split into $n + 1$ peaks:
- The –CH$_3$ signal is split into a 1:2:1 triplet because it has two neighbouring protons.
- The –CH$_2$– signal is split into a 1:3:3:1 quartet because it has three neighbouring protons.
- If there were a group with one neighbouring proton, then its signal would be split into a 1:1 doublet, but there is no such signal in ethanol.

The –OH proton appears as a singlet, devoid of any splitting. The –OH group is next to a –CH$_2$ group, so spin–spin coupling should produce a triplet for the OH signal. However, the –OH group is weakly acidic, so the proton ionises rapidly and transfers to other ethanol molecules and to water molecules. The –OH absorptions of this type are decoupled by this fast proton exchange and no splitting occurs.

The position of the –OH signal in an NMR spectrum can vary. The signal can be identified by the addition of D$_2$O: the –OH group becomes an –OD group and the –OH signal disappears from the spectrum.

A molecule such as ethane-1,2-diol, HOCH$_2$CH$_2$OH, will produce two singlets with peak areas in a ratio of 2:1. The –OH groups do not cause splitting and the two –CH$_2$– groups are chemically equivalent, so they do not couple.

Questions
&
Answers

These questions are similar in style and content to those that you can expect in Unit Test 4. They have been designed to test all the key facts and concepts covered in Module 4.

Unit Test 4 is divided into sections A and B. Section A questions are structured, with spaces at the end of each question part for your response. Section B usually contains a longer question, which is also divided into sections. It is effectively a long structured question, but with no spaces between each section for you to write your answer.

All the questions in this Question and Answer section are structured, without answer spaces. If a question is worth 12 marks, then you should expect to write no more than 12 sentences. The marking scheme identifies 12 key words or phrases that must be present for you to score the 12 marks.

The questions are worth 30 marks. In Unit Test 4 it is rare to find one question concentrating on one topic. However, these 30 marks could represent three separate structured questions, each worth 10 marks, from separate papers. The important point is that if you score well in each test, then you can be confident that you understand the topic.

Examiner's comments
Grade-A answers are provided for all questions. These are followed by examiner's comments (preceded by the icon), which point out common errors. They also suggest alternative answers that are acceptable and ways of remembering key points.

In order to use this section effectively, you should:
- make sure you have revised the topic thoroughly before you attempt the question
- read the question carefully and then answer it under test conditions
- use the grade-A answer to assess the quality of your answer — the grade-A answer has been marked by an examiner, with ticks placed where the marks are scored
- read through the examiner's comments to see the common errors made by candidates and tips for improving your answers
- never underestimate the help of your teacher — if you do not understand some of the points made in the answers or the examiner's comments, then ask your teacher (or other students) to explain
- make sure that you concentrate on your weak areas when revising rather than on the topics that you understand

In addition to this guide, use as much material from the AQA exam board as possible. Answer as many past paper questions as you can and then use the mark schemes to grade your answers and analyse your mistakes. As a rough guide, you need to score 80% for a grade A, 70% for a grade B and 60% for a grade C.

Question 1

Kinetics

(a) The reaction of peroxodisulphate(VI) ions and iodide ions was investigated by carrying out three separate experiments at constant temperature.

$$S_2O_8^{2-} + 2I^- \longrightarrow 2SO_4^{2-} + I_2$$

Experiment	Initial concentration of $S_2O_8^{2-}$/mol dm^{-3}	Initial concentration of I$^-$/mol dm^{-3}	Initial rate/ mol dm^{-3} s^{-1}
A	0.01	0.20	4.1×10^{-6}
B	0.02	0.20	8.2×10^{-6}
C	0.02	0.40	1.64×10^{-5}

(i) Use the data to deduce the order with respect to the peroxodisulphate(VI) ions. (3 marks)

(ii) Use the data to deduce the order with respect to the iodide ions. (3 marks)

(iii) State the rate equation. (1 mark)

(iv) Calculate the rate constant and deduce its units. (3 marks)

(b) 2-bromo-2-methylpropane reacts with sodium hydroxide according to the following equation:

$$(CH_3)_3CBr + OH^- \longrightarrow (CH_3)_3COH + Br^-$$

The following data are the results of three experiments carried out at 25°C.

Experiment	Initial concentration of $(CH_3)_3CBr$/mol dm^{-3}	Initial concentration of OH$^-$/mol dm^{-3}	Initial rate of reaction/ mol dm^{-3} s^{-1}
1	0.01	0.2	3×10^{-3}
2	0.02	0.2	6×10^{-3}
3	0.04	0.4	1.2×10^{-2}

(i) State the order with respect to 2-bromo-2-methylpropane. (1 mark)

(ii) State the order with respect to hydroxide ions. (1 mark)

(iii) State the rate equation. (1 mark)

(iv) Calculate the rate constant at this temperature and state its units. (3 marks)

(v) Calculate the initial rate of the reaction when the initial concentration of $(CH_3)_3CBr$ is 0.035 mol dm^{-3} and the initial concentration of OH$^-$ is 0.30 mol dm^{-3}. (1 mark)

(vi) State the effect, if any, on the rate constant of increasing the concentration of $(CH_3)_3CBr$ at a fixed temperature. (1 mark)

(vii) State, then explain, how a change in temperature affects the rate constant. (4 marks)

(c) The initial rate of reaction between substances A and B was measured in a series of experiments and the following rate equation was deduced:

rate = $k[A]^2[B]$

(i) Complete the table below for the reaction between **A** and **B**. (5 marks)

Experiment	Concentration of A/mol dm^{-3}	Concentration of B/mol dm^{-3}	Initial rate/ mol dm^{-3} s^{-1}
1	0.02	0.02	1.2×10^{-4}
2	0.04	0.04	
3	0.04		2.4×10^{-4}
4	0.03	0.06	
5		0.04	7.2×10^{-4}
6	0.08	0.08	

(ii) Use the data from experiment 1 to deduce a value for the rate constant, k, and state its units. (3 marks)

Total: 30 marks

■ ■ ■

Grade-A answer to Question 1

(a) (i) First order with respect to $S_2O_8^{2-}$ ✓. In experiments A and B, doubling $[S_2O_8^{2-}]$ and keeping $[I^-]$ constant ✓ leads to a doubling of the reaction rate ✓.

🗩 When investigating the effect of $S_2O_8^{2-}$ on the reaction rate it is essential that you emphasise that the concentration of I^- remains constant.

(ii) First order with respect to I^- ✓. In experiments B and C, doubling $[I^-]$ and keeping $[S_2O_8^{2-}]$ constant ✓ leads to a doubling in the reaction rate ✓.

🗩 Similarly, when investigating the effect of I^- on the reaction rate you must emphasise that the concentration of $S_2O_8^{2-}$ remains constant.

(iii) rate $= k[S_2O_8^{2-}][I^-]$ ✓

🗩 In the rate equation you must include the square brackets to indicate concentration in mol dm^{-3}.

(iv) $k = \dfrac{\text{rate}}{[S_2O_8^{2-}][I^-]} = \dfrac{4.1 \times 10^{-6}}{0.01 \times 0.20}$ ✓ $= 2.05 \times 10^{-3}$ ✓ mol^{-1} dm^3 s^{-1} ✓

🗩 The correct answer with the correct units scores 3 marks. If the answer is incorrect you can still score 1 mark for rearranging the rate equation and 1 mark for showing the correct units. The calculation shown here uses the data from experiment A. Any of the experiments would give the same answer.

(b) (i) First order with respect to $(CH_3)_3CBr$ ✓

🗩 Only the statement 'first order' is required. Looking at experiments 1 and 2, doubling $[(CH_3)_3CBr]$ and keeping $[OH^-]$ constant leads to a doubling of the reaction rate.

(ii) Zero order with respect to OH^- ✓

📝 Only the statement 'zero order' is required. Looking at experiments 2 and 3, doubling $[(CH_3)_3CBr]$ leads to a doubling of the reaction rate to 1.2×10^{-2}, so doubling OH^- at the same time must have had no effect on the reaction rate.

(iii) rate $= k[(CH_3)_3CBr]$ ✓

📝 As OH^- is zero order, it does not appear in the rate equation.

(iv) $k = \dfrac{\text{rate}}{[(CH_3)_3CBr]} = \dfrac{3 \times 10^{-3}}{0.01}$ ✓ $= 0.3$ ✓ s^{-1} ✓

📝 The calculation of the rate constant with the correct units scores 3 marks. If the answer is incorrect you can still score 1 mark for rearranging the rate equation and 1 mark for showing the correct units of the rate constant.

(v) rate $= k[(CH_3)_3CBr] = 0.3 \times 0.035 = 0.0105 = 1.05 \times 10^{-2}\,mol\,dm^{-3}\,s^{-1}$ ✓

📝 An alternative method could be used to deduce the reaction rate. Comparing the data given with that in experiment 1, the concentration of $(CH_3)_3CBr$ has increased by a factor of 3.5. If it is first order, the increase in rate will be directly proportional to the increase in the concentration of $(CH_3)_3CBr$. This means that the rate is $3 \times 10^{-3} \times 3.5 = 1.05 \times 10^{-2}$.

(vi) Concentration has no effect on the rate constant ✓.

📝 The key point to remember here is that only temperature alters the rate constant.

(vii) The rate constant increases ✓ with an increase in temperature ✓ because an increased temperature increases the average kinetic energy ✓ of the particles, which leads to a greater collision frequency ✓. However, a more important factor is that more molecules now possess energy greater than the energy of activation ✓, leading to many more successful collisions ✓.

📝 There are six scoring points and four available marks. It would be useful to include the Maxwell–Boltzmann distribution curves to show the distribution of molecular energies at two different temperatures.

(c) (i)

Experiment	Concentration of A/mol dm⁻³	Concentration of B/mol dm⁻³	Initial rate/ mol dm⁻³ s⁻¹
1	0.02	0.02	1.2×10^{-4}
2	0.04	0.04	9.6×10^{-4} ✓
3	0.04	0.01 ✓	2.4×10^{-4}
4	0.03	0.06	8.1×10^{-4} ✓
5	0.035 ✓	0.04	7.2×10^{-4}
6	0.08	0.08	7.68×10^{-3} ✓

✎ Completing a table of initial concentrations and initial rates is a common task. Marks are awarded for the final answers and no explanations are required. Answers were achieved as follows:

- Experiment 2: the reaction is third order overall, so doubling the concentration of both reactants between experiments 1 and 2 will lead to a 2^3 increase in reaction rate, that is, $8 \times 1.2 \times 10^{-4} = 9.6 \times 10^{-4}$.
- Experiment 3: comparing experiments 1 and 3, doubling the concentration of A should produce a quadrupling in the rate of reaction, that is, 4.8×10^{-4}. However, the rate is only half this value at 2.4×10^{-4}, so the concentration of B must have been halved.
- Experiment 4: comparing experiments 1 and 4, the concentration of A has increased by a factor of 1.5, so the rate will increase by $(1.5)^2 = 2.25$. The concentration of B has increased by a factor of 3, so the rate should increase overall by a factor of $2.25 \times 3 = 6.75$. This means the final answer is $6.75 \times 1.2 \times 10^{-4} = 8.1 \times 10^{-4}$.
- Experiment 5: comparing experiments 1 and 5, doubling the concentration of B should lead to a doubling in the reaction rate to 2.4×10^{-4}. The final rate is three times this value at 7.2×10^{-4}. This means that the concentration of A has increased by $\sqrt{3} = 1.732$. The concentration of A is $0.02 \times 1.732 = 0.03464 = 0.035$.
- Experiment 6: comparing experiments 2 and 6, the concentration of both reactants has doubled. The rate will therefore increase by a factor of 8, so $8 \times 9.6 \times 10^{-4} = 7.68 \times 10^{-3}$.

(ii) $k = \dfrac{\text{rate}}{[A]^2[B]} = \dfrac{1.2 \times 10^{-4}}{0.02^2 \times 0.02}$ ✓ $= 15$ ✓ $\text{mol}^{-2}\,\text{dm}^6\,\text{s}^{-1}$ ✓

✎ If the answer is incorrect then 1 mark will be awarded for rearranging the rate equation and 1 mark for the correct units. The data for all the experiments should produce the same rate constant. For example:

Experiment 2: $k = \dfrac{9.6 \times 10^{-4}}{0.04^2 \times 0.04} = 15$

Experiment 3: $k = \dfrac{2.4 \times 10^{-4}}{0.04^2 \times 0.01} = 15$

The rate constant could have been used to complete the data table in part (i).

uestion

Equilibria

(a) When 1.0 mol of ethanol and 1.0 mol of ethanoic acid were mixed together at 20°C, the reaction mixture at equilibrium was found to contain 0.667 mol of ethyl ethanoate. The total volume of the reaction mixture was 0.1 dm³. The equation for the reaction is:

$$C_2H_5OH + CH_3COOH \rightleftharpoons CH_3COOC_2H_5 + H_2O$$

  (i) Write an expression for the equilibrium constant, K_c, for this reaction. (1 mark)

  (ii) Calculate the equilibrium concentrations, in mol dm⁻³, of ethyl ethanoate and ethanol in the reaction mixture. (2 marks)

  (iii) Calculate the value of K_c at this temperature. (2 marks)

  (iv) In a separate experiment, 0.6 mol of ethanoic acid, 0.5 mol of ethanol, 0.6 mol of ethyl ethanoate, 0.4 mol of water and a small amount of concentrated sulphuric acid were mixed together at 20°C. At equilibrium, only 0.4 mol of ethanoic acid remained. The total volume of the reaction mixture was 0.1 dm³. Calculate the value of K_c found in this experiment. (4 marks)

(b) Dinitrogen tetraoxide and nitrogen dioxide exist in the following equilibrium:

$$N_2O_4(g) \rightleftharpoons 2NO_2(g) \qquad \Delta H = +58 \text{ kJ mol}^{-1}$$

When 10.4 g of N_2O_4 was placed in a vessel of volume 4.50 dm³ at a fixed temperature, 5.20 g of NO_2 was produced at equilibrium under a pressure of 100 kPa.

  (i) Calculate:
- the number of moles of NO_2 at equilibrium
- the number of moles of N_2O_4 that reacted
- the original moles of N_2O_4
- the number of moles of N_2O_4 at equilibrium (4 marks)

  (ii) Write an expression for the equilibrium constant, K_c, for this reaction. Calculate the value of K_c and state its units. (4 marks)

  (iii) Write an expression for the equilibrium constant, K_p, for the above equilibrium. (1 mark)

  (iv) Calculate:
- the total number of moles of NO_2 and N_2O_4 in the equilibrium mixture
- the mole fraction of NO_2
- the mole fraction of N_2O_4
- the partial pressure of NO_2
- the partial pressure of N_2O_4 (5 marks)

  (v) Calculate the value of the equilibrium constant, K_p, and state its units. (3 marks)

  (vi) State the effect, if any, on both the yield of NO_2 and on the equilibrium constant, K_p, of increasing the pressure and of increasing the temperature. (4 marks)

Total: 30 marks

Grade-A answer to Question 2

(a) (i) $K_c = \dfrac{[CH_3COOC_2H_5][H_2O]}{[C_2H_5OH][CH_3COOH]}$ ✓

When writing an expression for K_c, you must remember that it is always the products divided by the reactants. The concentrations are in $mol\,dm^{-3}$ so the square brackets [ ] are essential.

(ii) Concentration of ethyl ethanoate $= \dfrac{0.667}{0.1} = 6.67\,mol\,dm^{-3}$ ✓

Concentration of ethanol $= \dfrac{(1 - 0.667)}{0.1} = 3.33\,mol\,dm^{-3}$ ✓

When using K_c in calculations, it is essential that the concentrations are expressed in $mol\,dm^{-3}$. $0.667\,mol$ in $0.1\,dm^3$ is a concentration of $6.67\,mol\,dm^{-3}$. In this reaction, ignoring the volume would not affect the final answer because the value of V (i.e. $0.1\,dm^3$) cancels out as there are equal numbers of particles on the two sides of the equation. However, in equilibria involving unequal numbers of reactant and product particles, the volume does not cancel out (see part (b) of this question).

(iii) $K_c = \dfrac{6.67 \times 6.67}{3.33 \times 3.33} = 4.01$ ✓ (no units) ✓

The equation shows that for every mole of $CH_3COOC_2H_5$ produced there will be the same number of moles of H_2O, so the top line of the K_c expression becomes 6.67×6.67. In a similar way, for every mole of ethanoic acid that reacts the same amount of ethanol reacts, so the bottom line of the K_c expression becomes 3.33×3.33. There are no units for K_c because there are the same number of particles on both sides of the equation.

(iv)

	C_2H_5OH +	CH_3COOH ⇌	$CH_3COOC_2H_5$ +	H_2O
Initial moles	0.5	0.6	0.6	0.4
Equilibrium moles	0.5 − x	0.6 − x	0.6 + x	0.4 + x

If 0.4 mol of CH_3COOH remains, then the value of x must be 0.2. ✓

Equilibrium moles	0.3	0.4	0.8	0.6 ✓

If the total volume of reaction mixture is $0.1\,dm^3$:

Equilibrium conc.	3	4	8	6 ✓

$K_c = \dfrac{8 \times 6}{3 \times 4} = 4.0$ ✓

This is a more difficult calculation, but the principle is the same as above. Start with the original concentrations and determine how much has reacted (i.e. the value of x). This gives you how much you need to subtract from ethanol and how much you need to add to the original concentrations of ethyl ethanoate and water. The final answer of 4.0 scores 4 marks. However, if this is incorrect, then marks would be awarded for the working out, as indicated by the ticks in the grade-A answer. You would expect the value of K_c to be the same in parts (iii) and (iv) because the reactions were carried out at the same temperature.

(b) (i) Moles of NO_2 at equilibrium $= \dfrac{5.2}{46} = 0.113$ ✓

Moles of N_2O_4 reacted $= \dfrac{0.113}{2} = 0.0565$ ✓

Original moles of $N_2O_4 = \dfrac{10.4}{92} = 0.113$ ✓

Moles of N_2O_4 at equilibrium $= 0.113 - 0.0565 = 0.0565$ ✓

📝 The key to this calculation is realising that when x amount of N_2O_4 breaks down it produces 2x amount of NO_2. So when 0.113 mol of NO_2 is produced, 0.113/2 (= 0.0565) mol of N_2O_4 has broken down.

(ii) $K_c = \dfrac{[NO_2]^2}{[N_2O_4]}$ ✓

$K_c = \dfrac{(0.113/4.5)^2}{0.0565/4.5}$ ✓ $= 0.0502 = 5.02 \times 10^{-2}$ ✓ $mol\,dm^{-3}$ ✓

📝 When calculating K_c, the most common mistake is to miss the total volume of the reaction vessel, which in this case is $4.5\,dm^3$. If you do not include this, your final answer will be $0.226\,mol\,dm^{-3}$ and the only marks you could score here would be for the K_c expression and its units.

(iii) $K_p = \dfrac{p(NO_2)^2}{p(N_2O_4)}$ ✓

📝 You must use round brackets ( ) in the K_p expression.

(iv) Total number of moles at equilibrium $= 0.113 + 0.0565 = 0.1695$ ✓

Mole fraction of $NO_2 = \dfrac{0.113}{0.1695} = 0.6667 = 0.67$ ✓

Mole fraction of $N_2O_4 = \dfrac{0.0565}{0.1695} = 0.3333 = 0.33$ ✓

Partial pressure of $NO_2 = 0.6667 \times 100 = 66.67 = 67\,kPa$ ✓

Partial pressure of $N_2O_4 = 33.33 = 33\,kPa$ ✓

📝 This question is more structured than many A2 questions. There are two definitions you must remember in order to make progress with this calculation.
- The mole fraction is the number of moles of a species in the equilibrium mixture divided by the total number of moles of all the reactants and all the products in the equilibrium mixture.
- The partial pressure is the mole fraction multiplied by the total pressure.

When you have calculated all the partial pressures for the species in equilibrium, add them together. They should equal the total pressure.

(v) $K_p = \dfrac{(66.67)^2}{(33.33)}$ ✓ $= 133.3$ ✓ kPa ✓

question

2 Common mistakes include not squaring 66.67 and not stating the units of K_p.

(vi) Increasing the pressure will decrease the yield of NO_2 ✓ but have no effect on K_p ✓.

Increasing the temperature will increase the yield of NO_2 ✓ and increase the value of K_p ✓.

2 Remember that concentration, temperature and pressure can all affect the yield of the product by shifting the equilibrium position. However, the only factor that alters K_p is temperature. In this case, an increase in pressure will cause the equilibrium to shift to the left-hand side because there are fewer particles on this side and this will reduce the pressure and oppose the change. Pressure does not alter K_p. The reaction is endothermic, so an increase in temperature causes the equilibrium to shift to the right-hand side to reduce the temperature and oppose the change. The ratio of products to reactants increases, so the value of K_p increases.

Acids and bases (I)

(a) (i) Define the term Brønsted–Lowry acid. (1 mark)

(ii) Define pH. (1 mark)

(iii) Hydrochloric acid reacts with water according to the following equation:

$$HCl + H_2O \rightleftharpoons H_3O^+ + Cl^-$$

Write out the equation and label each species as an acid or a base. (1 mark)

(iv) Calculate the pH of a $0.5\,mol\,dm^{-3}$ solution of hydrochloric acid. (1 mark)

(b) Apple juice has a pH of 3.52. It is assumed that apple juice contains a weak monoprotic acid, HA. A $25.0\,cm^3$ sample of apple juice was exactly neutralised by $28.5\,cm^3$ of $0.10\,mol\,dm^{-3}$ sodium hydroxide using a suitable indicator.

(i) Define the following terms when applied to an acid:

• weak

• monoprotic (2 marks)

(ii) Assuming that apple juice contains this single monoprotic acid, HA, calculate the molar concentration of the acid in the juice. (3 marks)

(iii) Use the pH value to determine the molar concentration of hydrogen ions in apple juice. (2 marks)

(iv) Explain the difference between the two results for parts (ii) and (iii). (1 mark)

(v) Write an expression for K_a for the dissociation of the weak acid, HA. (1 mark)

(vi) Calculate a value for K_a and include its units. (3 marks)

(vii) Suggest a suitable indicator for this titration. (1 mark)

(c) Values for the ionic product of water, K_w, at various temperatures are given below.

T/°C	0	50	100
K_w	0.114×10^{-14}	5.48×10^{-14}	51.3×10^{-14}

(i) Define K_w, state its value at 25°C and include its units. (3 marks)

(ii) What is the pH of pure water at 50°C? (3 marks)

(iii) What is the pH at the equivalence point during the titration of an aqueous solution of hydrochloric acid with sodium hydroxide at 50°C? (1 mark)

(iv) Is the dissociation of water ($H_2O(l) \longrightarrow H^+(aq) + OH^-(aq)$) exothermic or endothermic? Explain your answer using the data on K_w above. (3 marks)

(v) Use the data above to calculate the pH of a $0.1\,mol\,dm^{-3}$ solution of sodium hydroxide at 100°C. (3 marks)

Total: 30 marks

■ ■ ■

Grade-A answer to Question 3

(a) (i) Proton donor ✓

The term 'H$^+$ donor' is an acceptable answer. A lone pair acceptor is incorrect, as this is the definition of a *Lewis* acid.

question

(ii) pH = $-\log_{10}$[H$^+$(aq)] ✓

💡 The minimum acceptable answer is 'pH = –lg[H$^+$]'. The square brackets are absolutely essential in the definition because this indicates molar concentration of hydrogen ions, that is, mol dm^{-3}. If you want to define pH in words then 'the negative logarithm to base 10 of the molar hydrogen ion concentration' is acceptable, with the word 'molar' essential.

(iii) HCl + H$_2$O $\rightleftharpoons$ H$_3$O$^+$ + Cl$^-$
    acid   base   acid   base ✓

💡 You have to identify all four species as either an acid or a base to obtain the mark. Remember, H$^+$ transfer is reversible and H$_3$O$^+$ is the only species on the right-hand side of the equation that is capable of donating an H$^+$ ion, so it must be the acid. This equation is often simplified to HCl(aq) $\rightleftharpoons$ H$^+$(aq) + Cl$^-$(aq). However, this does not show the proton transfer.

(iv) pH = $-\log_{10}$0.5 = 0.30 ✓

💡 To achieve the correct answer, enter '0.5' then '=' on your calculator, followed by 'log', then '=' again, then change the sign using the '+/–' button.

(b) (i) Partially ionised in solution ✓; liberates one proton per molecule on dissociation ✓

💡 The terms 'partially' or 'slightly' and 'ionised' or 'dissociated' are acceptable. The term 'not fully' would be given no credit. Examples of monoprotic acids include HCl, HNO$_3$ and CH$_3$COOH, because each acid is capable of dissociating in solution to liberate one H$^+$ ion per molecule. H$_2$SO$_4$ is a diprotic acid and H$_3$PO$_4$ is a triprotic acid.

(ii) Moles of NaOH used = $\dfrac{MV}{1000}$ = $\dfrac{0.1 \times 28.5}{1000}$ = 2.85 × 10^{-3} ✓
Moles of acid HA in 25 cm^3 = 2.85 × 10^{-3} ✓

Moles of HA in 1 dm^3, i.e. [HA] = 2.85 × 10^{-3} × $\dfrac{1000}{25}$ = 0.114 mol dm^{-3} ✓

💡 The correct answer of 0.114 mol dm^{-3} scores 3 marks. However, always show your working, because marks can be gained for each stage of the calculation. There are three definite steps in this calculation: moles of alkali used; using the 1:1 ratio in the equation; and scaling up the number of moles to molar concentration.

(iii) pH = $-\log_{10}$[H$^+$(aq)], so [H$^+$(aq)] = 10^{-pH} ✓
[H$^+$(aq)] = 10$^{-3.52}$ = 3.02 × 10^{-4} mol dm^{-3} ✓

💡 Many students find it difficult to convert pH back to [H$^+$] using [H$^+$] = 10^{-pH}. It depends on the calculator that you are using, but the stages are as follows: enter '10' then 'x^y' followed by '3.52' and '+/–' and finally '='. Sometimes a calculator requires you to enter the negative sign before entering 3.52. The final answer should be 3.02 × 10^{-4}. If you press 'log' followed by '+/–' you will go back to 3.52.

(iv) The acid is weak. It is only partially ionised, so it liberates few H^+ ions in solution ✓.

The original concentration is $0.114\,mol\,dm^{-3}$ and the number of H^+ ions in solution is $3.02 \times 10^{-4}\,mol\,dm^{-3}$, so only about 0.3% of the acid has dissociated, making it a weak acid. However, all the H^+ ions react with NaOH.

(v) $K_a = \dfrac{[H^+][A^-]}{[HA]}$ ✓

Common mistakes include using round brackets instead of square brackets and trying to simplify the expression to

$$K_a = \frac{[H^+]^2}{[HA]}$$

The latter may be used in calculations but not as the expression for K_a.

(vi) $K_a = \dfrac{[H^+]^2}{[HA]} = \dfrac{(3.02 \times 10^{-4})^2}{0.114}$ ✓ $= 8.00 \times 10^{-7}$ ✓ $mol\,dm^{-3}$ ✓

In this calculation it is assumed that the equilibrium concentration of H^+ is equal to the equilibrium concentration of A^-, that is, $[H^+] = [A^-]$ (so it now becomes $[H^+]^2$). It is also assumed that the amount of dissociation of HA is so small that the original concentration of HA is equal to the equilibrium concentration of HA, that is, $[HA]_{orig} = [HA]_{eqm}$. In calculations of K_a, remember to include the units for K_a at the end.

(vii) Phenolphthalein ✓

When a weak acid is titrated with a strong alkali the equivalence point occurs at a pH of about 8, so you need to select an indicator that will change colour between pH 8 and 10, for example phenolphthalein, thymolphthalein and phenol red.

(c) (i) $K_w = [H^+(aq)][OH^-(aq)]$ ✓ $= 1 \times 10^{-14}$ ✓ $mol^2\,dm^{-6}$ ✓

It is essential that square brackets are included in the expression to show that concentrations are in $mol\,dm^{-3}$. The value of K_w at 25°C is stated in the specification and you must remember it.

(ii) $K_w = [H^+][OH^-] = [H^+]^2$ ✓

$[H^+] = \sqrt{5.48 \times 10^{-14}} = 2.34 \times 10^{-7}$ ✓

$pH = -\log_{10}(2.34 \times 10^{-7}) = 6.63$ ✓

This calculation depends on the fact that when water dissociates it produces 1 mole of H^+ for every 1 mole of OH^-, so $[H^+] = [OH^-]$, which can be simplified to $[H^+]^2$. A common mistake is to forget to take the square root of the $[H^+]$ concentration.

(iii) 6.63 ✓

At 50°C the neutral pH is 6.63. When HCl and NaOH completely react at the equivalence point, the pH of the solution is neutral.

(iv) Endothermic ✓. Increasing the temperature increases the value of K_w ✓. The equilibrium position shifts to the right-hand side ✓ in order to reduce the temperature and oppose the change, so the equilibrium must be endothermic in the forward direction.

✒ This answer depends upon your understanding of Le Chatelier's principle. If you make a wrong statement, that is, the reaction is exothermic, then you will lose all 3 marks.

(v) $K_w = [H^+][OH^-]$, $[H^+] = \dfrac{K_w}{[OH^-]}$ ✓

$[H^+] = \dfrac{51.3 \times 10^{-14}}{0.1} = 5.13 \times 10^{-12}$ ✓

$pH = -\log_{10} (5.13 \times 10^{-12}) = 11.29$ ✓

✒ A common mistake is to use the wrong value for K_w. At 100°C, the value of K_w is 51.3×10^{-14}. Again, the correct answer will score 3 marks. However, it is sensible to show your working because if your answer is incorrect you can still score marks for rearranging the K_w expression and calculating $[H^+]$.

Acids and bases (II)

(a) A 25 cm³ sample of ethanoic acid ($K_a = 1.76 \times 10^{-5}$ mol dm⁻³) is titrated with a 0.15 mol dm⁻³ solution of sodium hydroxide. The equivalence point occurs at pH 8 and the volume of sodium hydroxide added at this point is 20.45 cm³.

  (i) Suggest a suitable indicator that could be used to detect the end point of the titration. (1 mark)

  (ii) Explain the difference between the terms 'equivalence point' and 'end point'. (2 marks)

  (iii) Use the information on the equivalence point to determine the original concentration of the ethanoic acid. (3 marks)

  (iv) Calculate the pH of the acid before the addition of any sodium hydroxide. (3 marks)

  (v) Calculate the pH of the solution after the addition of 10 cm³ of sodium hydroxide. (5 marks)

  (vi) Calculate the pH of the solution after the addition of 40 cm³ of sodium hydroxide. (5 marks)

(b) (i) Explain what is meant by the term 'buffer solution'. (2 marks)

  (ii) Give an example of a basic buffer. (2 marks)

  (iii) Explain how an equimolar solution of nitrous acid (HNO_2) and sodium nitrite ($NaNO_2$) is able to maintain a constant pH on the addition of small amounts of sodium hydroxide. (3 marks)

  (iv) Calculate the pH of a buffer solution made by mixing together 10.0 cm³ of 1.00 mol dm⁻³ nitrous acid with 20.0 cm³ of 2.00 mol dm⁻³ sodium nitrite solution. (K_a of nitrous acid = 4.57×10^{-4} mol dm⁻³) (4 marks)

Total: 30 marks

■ ■ ■

Grade-A answer to Question 4

(a) (i) Phenolphthalein ✓

📝 Any indicator that changes between pH 8 and 10 would be suitable, so phenol red and thymolphthalein are also acceptable answers.

  (ii) The equivalence point occurs when stoichiometric amounts (equal numbers of moles) of acid and base are mixed together ✓. The end point occurs when the indicator changes colour ✓.

📝 Any expression that implies that equal numbers of moles of acid and alkali have been mixed is acceptable for the definition of the equivalence point. Indicators are chosen so that the colour change (end point) coincides with the equivalence point.

  (iii) Moles of NaOH added $= \dfrac{MV}{1000} = \dfrac{0.15 \times 20.45}{1000} = 3.0675 \times 10^{-3}$ ✓

  Moles of CH_3COOH in 25 cm³ $= 3.0675 \times 10^{-3}$ ✓

  $[CH_3COOH] = 3.0675 \times 10^{-3} \times \dfrac{1000}{25} = 0.1227 = 0.123$ mol dm⁻³ ✓

4

question

💡 The correct answer scores 3 marks. Remember your working, because if your final answer is incorrect then credit will be given for showing any of the three steps: moles of alkali added; using the 1:1 ratio in the equation; and scaling up the moles of acid to molar concentration.

(iv) $K_a = \dfrac{[CH_3COO^-][H^+]}{[CH_3COOH]} = \dfrac{[H^+]^2}{[CH_3COOH]}$ ✓

$[H^+] = \sqrt{K_a \times [CH_3COOH]} = \sqrt{1.76 \times 10^{-5} \times 0.1227} = 1.469 \times 10^{-3}$ ✓

$pH = -\log_{10}(1.469 \times 10^{-3}) = 2.83$ ✓

💡 The correct answer scores 3 marks. This calculation depends upon the assumption that the number of moles of H^+ equals the number of moles of CH_3COO^- (so the K_a expression is simplified to include $[H^+]^2$) and that the original concentration of CH_3COOH is the same as the concentration of CH_3COOH at equilibrium (because only a tiny amount of the CH_3COOH has dissociated). This means the expression $[H^+] = \sqrt{K_a \times [CH_3COOH]}$ can be used to calculate pH. A common answer is 5.67 (failing to take the square root) and this scores only 2 marks.

(v) Original moles of $CH_3COOH = \dfrac{MV}{1000} = \dfrac{0.1227 \times 25}{1000} = 3.0675 \times 10^{-3}$

Moles of NaOH added $= \dfrac{0.15 \times 10}{1000} = 1.5 \times 10^{-3}$ ✓

Moles of CH_3COO^- formed $= 1.5 \times 10^{-3}$ ✓

Moles of CH_3COOH remaining $= (3.0675 \times 10^{-3}) - (1.5 \times 10^{-3}) = 1.5675 \times 10^{-3}$ ✓

$K_a = \dfrac{[CH_3COO^-][H^+]}{[CH_3COOH]}$, so $[H^+] = K_a \dfrac{[CH_3COOH]}{[CH_3COO^-]}$

$[H^+] = 1.76 \times 10^{-5} \times \dfrac{1.5675 \times 10^{-3}}{1.5 \times 10^{-3}} = 1.8392 \times 10^{-5}$ ✓

$pH = -\log_{10}(1.8392 \times 10^{-5}) = 4.7353 = 4.74$ ✓

💡 This is probably one of the most difficult calculations at A2 and only the most able candidates will score full marks on this section. The correct answer of 4.74 scores 5 marks but if the final answer is incorrect then credit will be given for the working.

(vi) Moles of $CH_3COOH = 3.0675 \times 10^{-3}$

Moles of NaOH added $= \dfrac{0.15 \times 40}{1000} = 6 \times 10^{-3}$ ✓

Excess moles of NaOH $= (6 \times 10^{-3}) - (3.0675 \times 10^{-3}) = 2.9325 \times 10^{-3}$ ✓

Total volume of the solution $= 25 + 40 = 65 \, cm^3$

$[OH^-] = 2.9325 \times 10^{-3} \times \dfrac{1000}{65} = 0.0451 \, mol \, dm^{-3}$ ✓

$[H^+] = \dfrac{K_w}{[OH^-]} = \dfrac{1.0 \times 10^{-14}}{0.0451} = 2.217 \times 10^{-13}$ ✓

$pH = -\log_{10}(2.217 \times 10^{-13}) = 12.65 = 12.7$ ✓

💡 This is another difficult calculation. Again, the correct answer scores 5 marks. There are definite steps to remember in calculations of this type: moles of acid added; moles of alkali added; excess alkali (or sometimes excess acid); total volume of solution formed; molar concentration of OH^-; using K_w to determine the molar concentration of H^+; and using $-\log_{10}[H^+]$ to determine pH. The most common mistake is failing to scale up OH^- to molar concentration. If you fail to do this then you will get $[H^+] = 3.41 \times 10^{-12}$ and pH = 11.47 — this is an incorrect answer but you will still be awarded 3 out of a possible 5 marks.

(b) (i) A buffer solution resists changes in pH ✓ on the addition of small amounts of acid or alkali ✓.

✍ The two key points in this definition are 'resisting pH change' and 'adding small amounts'.

(ii) Ammonia ✓ and ammonium chloride ✓

✍ Any weak alkali and its salt can be used as an example of a basic buffer, for example methylamine and methylammonium chloride.

(iii) The following equilibrium exists between nitrous acid and sodium nitrite:
$$HNO_2 \rightleftharpoons H^+ + NO_2^- \checkmark$$
The OH^- ions that are added react with the H^+ ions ✓. However, the pH does not change because some HNO_2 dissociates and the equilibrium position shifts to the right ✓ to replace the H^+ ions.

✍ The key point is that the buffer solution contains a large amount of undissociated acid (HNO_2) and a large amount of the anion NO_2^- (which has come from the salt). Addition of OH^- removes H^+ but the equilibrium position moves to the right to replace the H^+. If H^+ is added it reacts with the NO_2^- and the equilibrium position shifts to the left-hand side and removes the added H^+. In both cases, the pH change has been resisted.

(iv) $K_a = \dfrac{[H^+][NO_2^-]}{[HNO_2]}$ ✓

$$\text{Moles } HNO_2 = \frac{1 \times 10}{1000} = 0.01$$

$$\text{Moles } NaNO_2 = \frac{2 \times 20}{1000} = 0.04$$

$$\therefore K_a = \frac{[H^+] \times 0.04}{0.01} = 4.57 \times 10^{-4} \checkmark$$

$$[H^+] = \frac{4.57 \times 10^{-4}}{4} = 1.1425 \times 10^{-4} \checkmark; \text{ pH} = -\log_{10}(1.1425 \times 10^{-4}) = 3.94 \checkmark$$

✍ An alternative method would be as follows:
$K_a = 4.57 \times 10^{-4}$, so $pK_a = 3.34$ ✓
$$pH = pK_a + \log_{10}\frac{[\text{salt}]}{[\text{acid}]} \checkmark = 3.34 + \log_{10}\frac{0.04}{0.01} \checkmark = 3.34 + \log 4 = 3.94 \checkmark$$

uestion 5

Nomenclature and isomerism in organic chemistry (I)

(a) Explain the terms 'structural isomerism' and 'stereoisomerism'.   (5 marks)

(b) Name the following compounds.

(i)

H_3C—CH, CH₃, CH—CH₃, H₃C

(ii)

H_3C—C, CH₃, C—H, H₃C

(iii)

H_3C—CH, H, CH—CH₃, Br

(iv)

H_3C—C—CH₃, OH, CH₃

(v)

CH₃

(vi)

CH₃

(vii)

CH₃

(viii)

OH

(ix)

O

(x) H_3C—CH₂—O—CH₂—CH₃

(xi)

H_3C—C, H, C—C, O, H, H

(xii)

H_3C—CH₂, H_3C—CH₂, C=O

(12 marks)

(c) Draw and name the *four* isomeric esters of molecular formula $C_4H_8O_2$.   (8 marks)

(d) Draw and name the *two* carboxylic acids that also have the molecular formula $C_4H_8O_2$.   (4 marks)

(e) The structure of warfarin is shown below. Use an asterisk (*) to label the chiral centre present in this molecule.

O, C=O, C=C, CH, CH₂, CH₃, OH, C=O

(1 mark)

Total: 30 marks

Grade-A answer to Question 5

(a) Structural isomerism occurs when molecules have the same molecular formula ✓ but different structural formulae ✓. Stereoisomerism occurs when molecules have the same molecular formula ✓ and the same structural formula ✓ but a different spatial arrangement of their bonds ✓. There are two types — geometric and optical ✓.

📝 There are six key points, of which five must be covered for 5 marks to be awarded. In the definition of stereoisomerism, if the term 'same structural formula' is missing, then the mark for different spatial arrangement of bonds will not be awarded.

(b) (i) 2,3-dimethylbutane ✓
(ii) 2-methylbut-2-ene ✓
(iii) 2-bromobutane ✓
(iv) 2-methylpropan-2-ol ✓
(v) Methylcyclohexane ✓
(vi) Methylbenzene ✓
(vii) 1-methylcyclohexene ✓
(viii) Cyclohexanol ✓
(ix) Cyclohexanone ✓
(x) Ethoxyethane ✓
(xi) *trans*-but-2-enal ✓
(xii) Pentan-3-one ✓

📝 In the unit test you will be asked to name at least one compound.

(c)

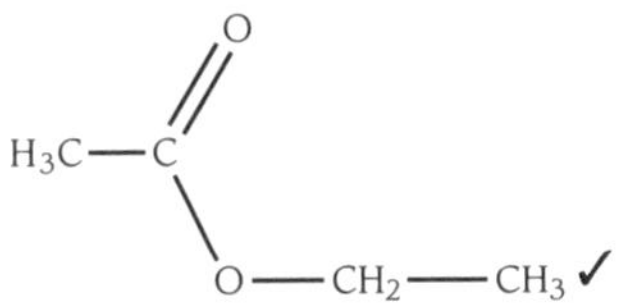

Ethyl ethanoate ✓

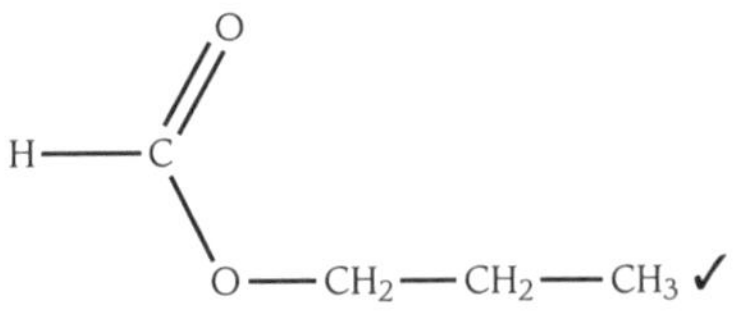

Propyl methanoate ✓

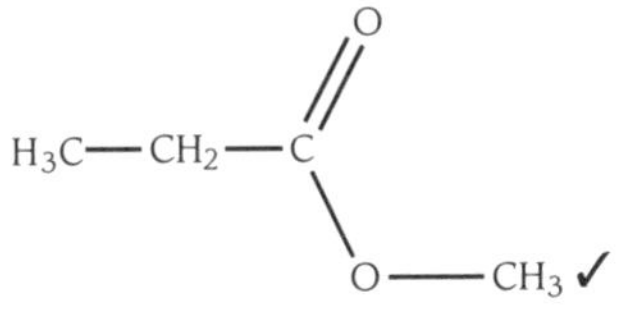

Methyl propanoate ✓

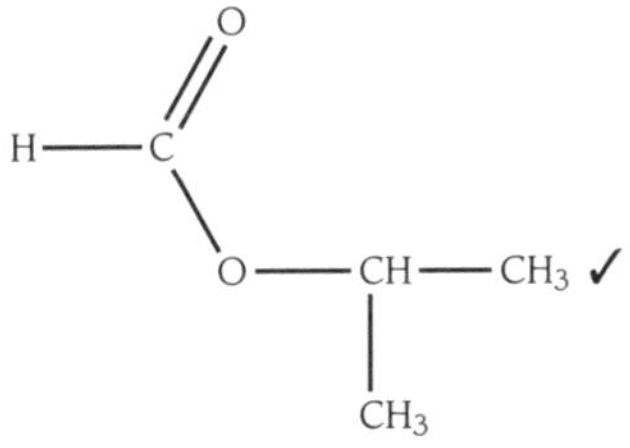

Methylethyl methanoate ✓

📝 When drawing esters, remember to start with the functional group –COO–, then place the remaining carbons each side of this group. You cannot attach hydrogen to the oxygen because this would produce a carboxylic acid. The most difficult ester to identify and name is the branched ester. Only the most able candidates will score this mark.

(d)

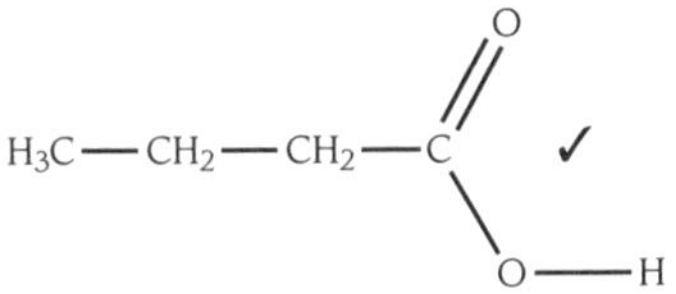

Butanoic acid ✓

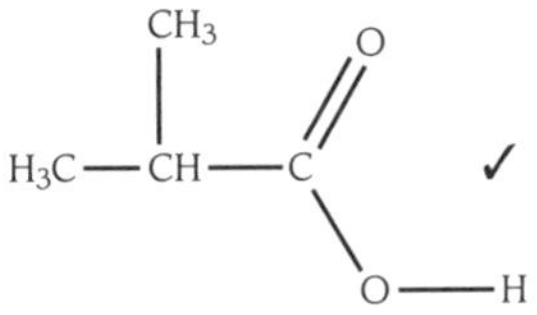

Methylpropanoic acid ✓

5

question

> Always draw the straight-chain carboxylic acid with the –COOH at the end of the chain, then consider if branching is possible in the hydrocarbon chain.

(e)

> This type of question, involving more complex molecules, is becoming quite common because it tests your ability to apply basic principles to new and unusual situations. You have to look for a carbon atom with four different groups attached.

Nomenclature and isomerism in organic chemistry (II)

(a) Draw all the structural isomers of C_4H_9Br. State the name of the isomer that is capable of exhibiting optical isomerism, draw the two enantiomers of this compound and explain how these two isomers could be distinguished from each other. (10 marks)

(b) (i) Draw the two geometric isomers of but-2-enal and label them *cis* or *trans*. (4 marks)

(ii) Draw the two structural isomers of but-2-enal that do not exhibit geometric isomerism but still contain an alkene and an aldehyde functional group. (2 marks)

(c) Name the following compounds.

(i)

H_3C — C — C≡N
with OH above C and H below C

(ii)

H_3C — CH
with CH₃ above, and below CH: C=O with H₂N attached

(iii)

H_3C — CH
with NH₂ above, and below CH: C=O with HO attached

(iv)

H_3C—CH_2—CH_2—NH_2

(v)

H — C
with O double bond above, and O—CH_2—CH_2—CH_3 below

(vi)

H_3C—(benzene ring)—CH_3

(vii)

(substituted benzene ring with CH₃ top, CH₃ right, H₃C bottom left)

(viii)

H_3C—CH_2—CH_2—C
with O double bond above and Cl below

(ix) HC≡CH₂
(vinyl-substituted benzene ring)

(9 marks)

(d) The structures of three compounds, which are found in perfumes, are shown below.

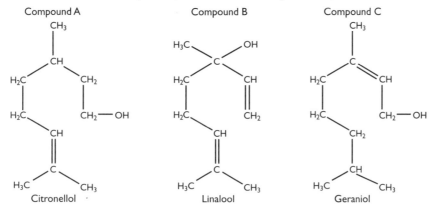

Compound A — Citronellol
Compound B — Linalool
Compound C — Geraniol

93

Use the letters **A, B** and **C** to answer the questions below.
(i) Which of these compounds are structural isomers?
(ii) Which of these compounds will exhibit geometric isomerism?
(iii) Which of these compounds will exhibit optical isomerism?

(5 marks)

Total: 30 marks

■ ■ ■

Grade-A answer to Question 6

(a) $H_3C-CH_2-CH_2-CH_2-Br$ ✓ $H_3C-CH-CH_2-CH_3$ ✓
                                                            |
                                                            Br

$H_3C-\overset{\overset{\displaystyle CH_3}{|}}{\underset{\underset{\displaystyle Br}{|}}{C}}-CH_3$ ✓ $H_3C-\overset{\overset{\displaystyle CH_3}{|}}{CH}-CH_2-Br$ ✓

The compound capable of exhibiting optical isomerism is 2-bromobutane ✓. The two enantiomers of 2-bromobutane are:

Mirror

The enantiomers can be distinguished by their ability to rotate ✓ plane-polarised light ✓ in opposite directions ✓.

💡 To identify all four isomers you must adopt a logical approach. Always start with the longest unbranched hydrocarbon chain and position the bromine atom at carbon 1. Then try to place it in different positions along the chain. You will find that only bromine at number 2 produces a different structural isomer. You then need to produce structural isomers that have branched hydrocarbon chains and in which the bromine atom can be placed on the first or the second carbon atom. If you draw more than four structural isomers, full marks will not be awarded: four correct isomers and one extra isomer will score 3 marks, four correct isomers and two extra isomers will score 2 marks and so on.

Only 2-bromobutane contains a carbon atom with four different groups attached. When drawing the enantiomers you must emphasise the importance of the asymmetric carbon atom and show the four different groups attached in a tetrahedral fashion. Enantiomers have the same chemical and physical properties but they differ in their effect on plane-polarised light. Using the word 'reflect' rather than 'rotate' is a common mistake.

(b) (i)

trans ✓ cis ✓

📝 In order to exhibit geometric isomerism, the carbon atoms attached to the double bond must have different groups attached.

(ii)

📝 The two structural isomers that do not exhibit geometric isomerism have two hydrogen atoms attached to one of the carbon atoms.

(c) (i) 2-hydroxypropanenitrile ✓
(ii) 2-methylpropanamide ✓
(iii) 2-aminopropanoic acid ✓
(iv) Propylamine ✓
(v) Propyl methanoate ✓

(vi) 1,4-dimethylbenzene ✓
(vii) 1,2,4-trimethylbenzene ✓
(viii) Butanoyl chloride ✓
(ix) Phenylethene ✓

📝 In the unit test you will be asked to name at least one compound.

(d) (i) Compounds A ✓ and C ✓

📝 You have been asked to apply the basic principles to three unusual compounds that you will not have met before. Compounds A and C are structural isomers because they have the same molecular formula ($C_{10}H_{20}O$) but different structural formulae. Compound B has a molecular formula of $C_{10}H_{18}O$.

(ii) Compound C only ✓

📝 Compound C has four different groups attached to the carbon atoms involved in the carbon–carbon double bond and will exhibit geometric isomerism. Compounds A and B will not exhibit geometric isomerism. Compound A has two methyl groups attached to a carbon atom involved in the carbon–carbon double bond. Compound B has two methyl groups attached to a carbon atom involved in one carbon–carbon double bond and two hydrogen atoms attached to a carbon atom in the other double bond.

(iii) Compounds A ✓ and B ✓

📝 Compounds A and B both possess asymmetric carbon atoms, that is, a carbon atom with four different groups attached, but compound C possesses no such carbon atom.

Question 7

Aldehydes and ketones

(a) Consider the carbonyl compounds labelled A to C below.

Compound A

Compound B

Compound C

(i) Name compounds A, B and C. (3 marks)

(ii) Write an equation, showing clearly the structure of the final product, for the reaction of compound A with HCN, compound B with acidified $K_2Cr_2O_7$ and compound C with $NaBH_4$. (6 marks)

(iii) Write an equation for the oxidation of the appropriate alcohol to produce compound A. (2 marks)

(iv) State which of the compounds labelled A to C would react with ammoniacal silver nitrate (Tollens' reagent). Explain why they can react and state the observations for a positive result. (4 marks)

(v) What colour change would be observed if compound C were warmed with Fehling's solution? (1 mark)

(vi) State the name of, then draw, the mechanism for the reaction of compound B with HCN. (4 marks)

(b) Compound X has the following structure:

(i) Name compound X. (1 mark)

(ii) Draw a geometric isomer of compound X. (1 mark)

(iii) Write equations for the reactions of compound X with Br_2 and with HCN. (2 marks)

(iv) Give simple structural formulae for the products formed when compound X is:

- reduced with $NaBH_4$
- reduced with H_2 in the presence of a nickel catalyst
- oxidised with acidified $K_2Cr_2O_7$ (3 marks)

(v) Draw the mechanism for the reaction of compound X with $NaBH_4$. (3 marks)

Total: 30 marks

Grade-A answer to Question 7

(a) (i) A = butanone ✓; B = butanal ✓; C = methylpropanal ✓

💬 There is no need to include the numbers to indicate the position of the functional group. Compound A is a ketone and the C=O group can only occur at the 2 position. Compounds B and C are aldehydes and the CHO group is always numbered 1.

(ii)

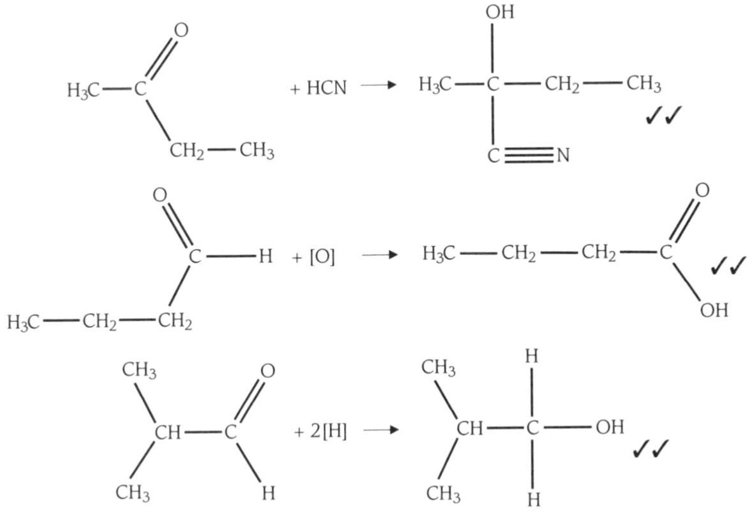

💬 In each case there is 1 mark for the product and 1 mark for balancing the equation with the appropriate symbol. When compound B is oxidised [O] is used for the oxidising agent and when compound C is reduced [H] is used for the reducing agent. Do not try to include $K_2Cr_2O_7$ and $NaBH_4$ in your equations.

(iii)

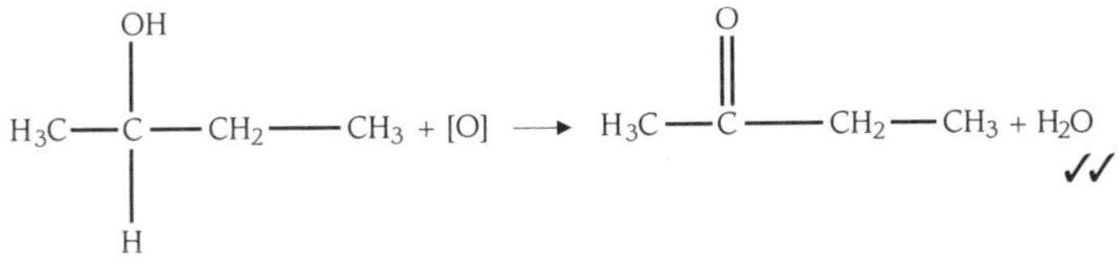

💬 There is 1 mark for the structure of the alcohol and 1 mark for the equation. Again, use [O] for the oxidising agent. The most common mistake is the omission of H_2O from the balanced equation.

(iv) B ✓ and C ✓. Aldehydes can be further oxidised to a carboxylic acid ✓. A silver mirror is produced ✓.

💬 The ability of aldehydes to be readily oxidised by mild oxidising agents provides the main method of distinguishing between aldehydes and ketones.

(v) Blue solution to red precipitate ✓

💬 Fehling's solution is the alternative test, distinguishing between aldehydes and ketones. The red precipitate produced is copper(I) oxide.

(vi) Nucleophilic addition ✓

💡 The mechanism must be drawn carefully. The 3 marks are for the curly arrows shown, but these will not be awarded if the lone pairs on the cyanide ion and on the oxygen in the intermediate structure are not shown.

(b) (i) But-2-enal ✓

💡 But-2-enal is an acceptable answer. However, if you name it as the geometric isomer then it *must* be named as *trans*-but-2-enal.

(ii)

💡 Geometric isomerism occurs due to the non-rotation of the carbon–carbon double bond and the *cis*-isomer is the other alternative.

(iii) $CH_3CH=CHCHO + Br_2 \longrightarrow CH_3CHBrCHBrCHO$ ✓
$CH_3CH=CHCHO + HCN \longrightarrow CH_3CH=CHCH(OH)CN$ ✓

💡 It is quite common to see questions on the chemistry of compounds with more than one functional group. You must treat these functional groups separately. In the first reaction it is an alkene reacting with bromine and the rest of the molecule remains unchanged. In the second reaction it is an aldehyde reacting with HCN and the alkene double bond is unchanged. Remember, HCN is a nucleophilic reagent because the initial attack is by a cyanide ion (CN⁻, an electron pair donor) on the electron-deficient carbon atom of the C=O group. In contrast, HBr is an electrophilic reagent because the electron-deficient hydrogen of the HBr readily accepts an electron pair from the carbon–carbon double bond of the alkene.

(iv) $CH_3CH=CHCH_2OH$ ✓
$CH_3CH_2CH_2CH_2OH$ ✓
$CH_3CH=CHCOOH$ ✓

💡 Reduction products depend on the reagent used. $NaBH_4$ only attacks carbonyl compounds, whereas hydrogen attacks both carbonyls and alkenes. When trying to predict the oxidation products using $K_2Cr_2O_7$, treat but-2-enal like any other aldehyde. Ignore the rest of the molecule, because it will remain unchanged.

(v)

Be careful when drawing mechanisms. The 3 marks will be awarded for the curly arrows provided that the lone pairs are included on the H^- ion and on the oxygen atom in the intermediate structure.

Carboxylic acids and esters

(a) (i) Draw two isomeric esters with the molecular formula $C_3H_6O_2$.   (2 marks)

(ii) For each ester, write an equation for its preparation from suitable reagents. State the catalyst needed for both reactions.   (5 marks)

(iii) For either one of these esters, predict the products of its alkaline hydrolysis.   (2 marks)

(iv) State the name and draw the structural formula of the carboxylic acid that is isomeric with the two esters in part (i).   (2 marks)

(v) Write equations for the reaction of the carboxylic acid shown in part (iv) with:
- sodium hydroxide
- sodium carbonate
- propan-2-ol   (3 marks)

(b) The structure of methylethyl methanoate is shown below:

Methylethyl methanoate

(i) Deduce the molecular and empirical formulae of the ester.   (2 marks)

(ii) Draw and name three other esters that are isomeric with this compound.   (6 marks)

(iii) Write an equation for the alkaline hydrolysis of methylethyl methanoate, showing clearly the structure of each product.   (2 marks)

(iv) Name the carboxylic acids that are isomeric with the ester methylethyl methanoate.   (2 marks)

(c) 2-hydroxypropanoic acid, obtained from sour milk, has the ability to rotate plane-polarised light.

(i) Draw the structural formula of this acid and explain why it has this property.   (2 marks)

(ii) Predict the structure of the compounds formed when 2-hydroxypropanoic acid reacts, in the presence of a strong acid catalyst, separately with:
- ethanol
- ethanoic acid   (2 marks)

Total: 30 marks

■ ■ ■

Grade-A answer to Question 8

(a) (i)

☑ There are only two possible answers. When drawing esters, always start by drawing the functional group:

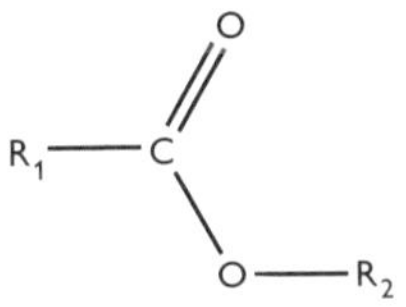

R_1 can be hydrogen or an alkyl group and R_2 can be an alkyl group. You must not make R_2 hydrogen, because this would be a carboxylic acid.

(ii) $CH_3COOH + CH_3OH \longrightarrow CH_3COOCH_3 + H_2O$ ✓✓
$HCOOH + CH_3CH_2OH \longrightarrow HCOOCH_2CH_3 + H_2O$ ✓✓
Concentrated sulphuric acid is the catalyst ✓.

☑ The principle to apply here is that an alcohol reacts with an acid to produce an ester and water.

(iii) $CH_3COO^-Na^+$ ✓ and CH_3OH ✓ or $HCOO^-Na^+$ ✓ and C_2H_5OH ✓

☑ The basic principle is that when an ester undergoes alkaline hydrolysis the bond breaks as shown below:

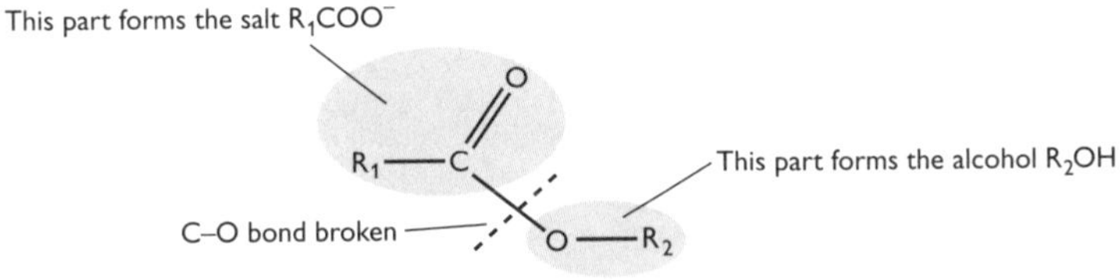

This part forms the salt R_1COO^-

R_1—C

C–O bond broken

This part forms the alcohol R_2OH

(iv) Propanoic acid ✓, CH_3CH_2COOH ✓

☑ There is only one carboxylic acid with the molecular formula $C_3H_6O_2$.

(v) $CH_3CH_2COOH + NaOH \longrightarrow CH_3CH_2COO^-Na^+ + H_2O$ ✓
$2CH_3CH_2COOH + Na_2CO_3 \longrightarrow 2CH_3CH_2COO^-Na^+ + CO_2 + H_2O$ ✓
$CH_3CH_2COOH + CH_3CH(OH)CH_3 \longrightarrow CH_3CH_2COOCH(CH_3)_2 + H_2O$ ✓

☑ Propanoic acid behaves as a typical acid, forming a salt and water with sodium hydroxide and liberating carbon dioxide from sodium carbonate solution. In the final reaction it is reacting with an alcohol to form an ester and water. The final product is a branched ester because the alcohol attaches to the carboxylic acid using the oxygen atom. The branched ester must be shown in the equation to gain the final mark.

(b) (i) The molecular formula is $C_4H_8O_2$ ✓ and the empirical formula is C_2H_4O ✓.

☑ The molecular formula is the actual number of atoms of each element in the compound and the empirical formula is the simplest possible ratio of the atoms of each element in the compound.

(ii)

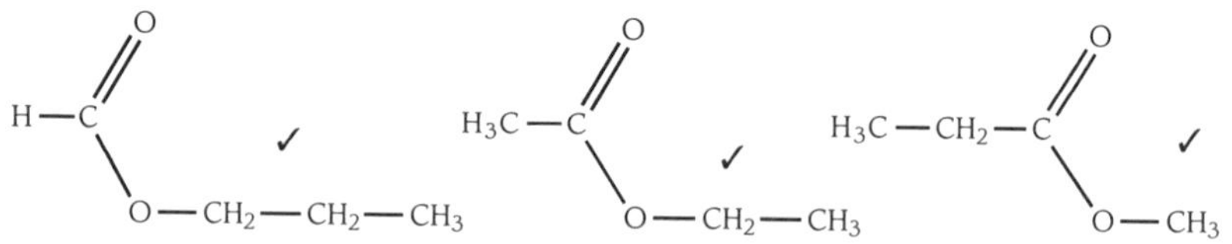

| Propyl methanoate ✓ | Ethyl ethanoate ✓ | Methyl propanoate ✓ |

When naming esters, remember which part is derived from the alcohol and which part is derived from the acid; for example:

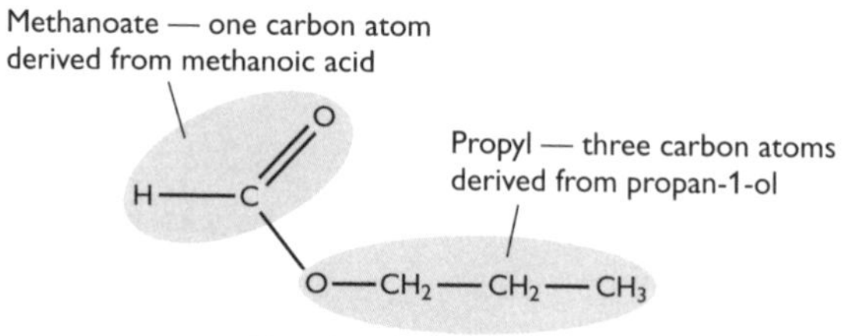

Methanoate — one carbon atom derived from methanoic acid

Propyl — three carbon atoms derived from propan-1-ol

Propyl methanoate

(iii)

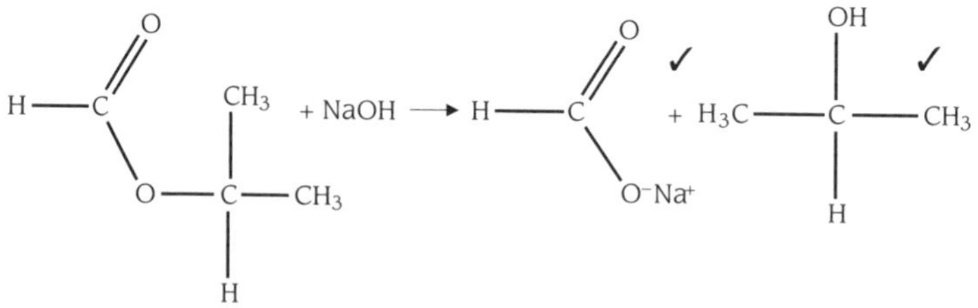

The important point to recognise here is that the ester is branched, so when the C–O bond breaks it leads to the formation of propan-2-ol and not propan-1-ol.

(iv) Butanoic acid ✓ and methylpropanoic acid ✓

The common mistake here is to draw the structures when names are asked for.

(c) (i)

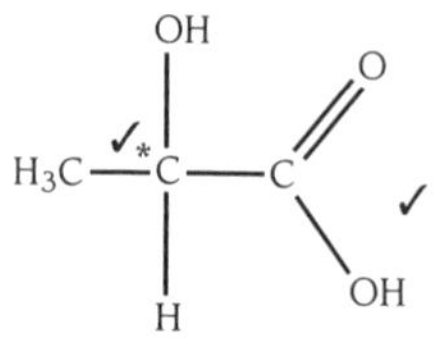

2-hydroxypropanoic acid is optically active because it is a chiral molecule, that is, the carbon shown with an asterisk is asymmetric because it has four different groups attached.

To be optically active, a molecule must possess a chiral centre, that is, an asymmetric carbon atom. There is 1 mark for drawing the structure and 1 mark for indicating where the chiral centre is in the molecule.

(ii) With ethanol:

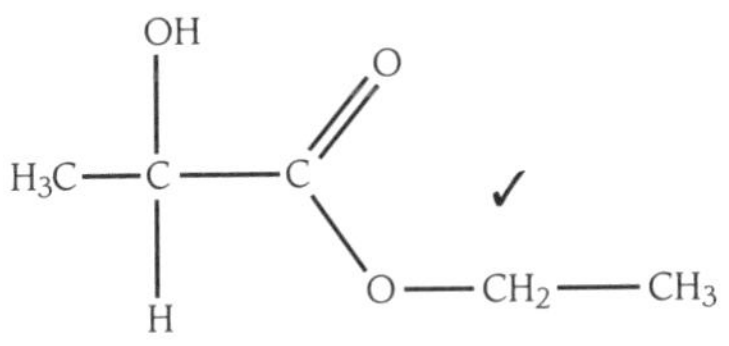

With ethanoic acid:

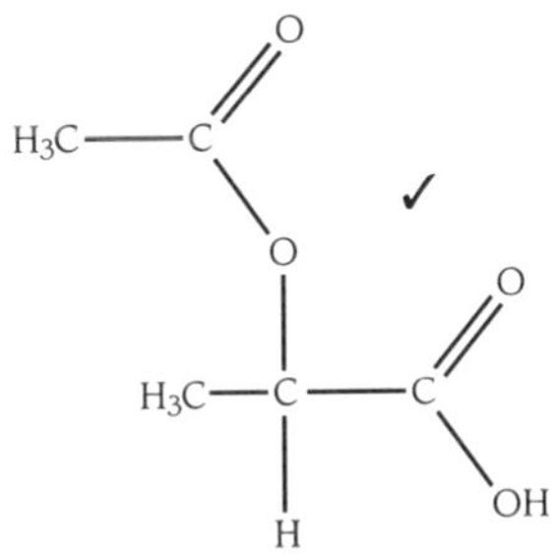

The compound 2-hydroxypropanoic acid contains an –OH group and a –COOH group. Each group can form an ester, depending on the reagent added. The –COOH group will react with ethanol to form an ester and the –OH group will react with ethanoic acid to form an ester.

Acylation

(a) (i) **Write an equation for the formation of ethyl ethanoate from ethanoyl chloride and ethanol.** (1 mark)

(ii) **Name and outline a mechanism for the reaction that takes place in part (i).** (5 marks)

(iii) **Suggest why the reaction in part (i) is a more efficient way of preparing ethyl ethanoate than the reaction between ethanoic acid and ethanol.** (2 marks)

(b) (i) **Write an equation for the reaction of propanoyl chloride with ethylamine.** (2 marks)

(ii) **Outline a mechanism for the reaction that takes place in part (i).** (4 marks)

(iii) **Suggest the structures of the acyl chlorides and amines used to produce the following amide derivatives X and Y:**

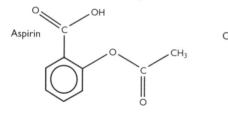

(4 marks)

(c) **The compound 2-hydroxybenzenecarboxylic acid can be converted into two products, aspirin and oil of wintergreen, which are used as medicines.**

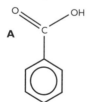

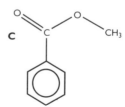

(i) **Write equations for the conversion of 2-hydroxybenzenecarboxylic acid into aspirin and oil of wintergreen.** (4 marks)

(ii) **State the name of the catalyst used in the production of oil of wintergreen.** (1 mark)

(iii) **State the name of an alternative reagent for the production of aspirin.** (1 mark)

(d) **Consider the compounds A to C.**

(i) **State the letter of the compound that will:**
- **react with hot sodium hydroxide to produce methanol as one of the products**
- **react with ammonia to produce an amide**
- **react with cold water to produce compound A** (3 marks)

(ii) Write equations to describe:
- the conversion of compound **A** into compound **D**
- the conversion of compound **B** into compound **E**

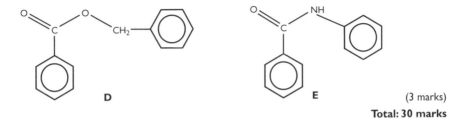

D   **E**   (3 marks)

Total: 30 marks

■ ■ ■

Grade-A answer to Question 9

(a) (i) $CH_3COCl + C_2H_5OH \longrightarrow CH_3COOC_2H_5 + HCl$ ✓

🖉 Acyl chlorides and alcohols react to produce an ester. The most common mistake is the omission of HCl from the equation.

(ii) Nucleophilic addition–elimination ✓

🖉 There is 1 mark for each of the curly arrows in the first stage, but you must show one lone pair on the oxygen atom of the alcohol to gain the second mark. For the third mark you must show the correct structure of the intermediate, the correct charges and two correct curly arrows. The fourth mark is for showing the loss of the H^+, with the curly arrow showing the electron pair returning to the oxygen.

(iii) It is not an equilibrium, so gives a better yield ✓. It requires no catalyst ✓.

🖉 Esterifications involving carboxylic acids and alcohols are equilibrium reactions, requiring heat and a catalyst. Acyl chlorides are more reactive than carboxylic acids because they possess two electron-withdrawing groups (C=O and C–Cl), making the carbon very electron deficient and susceptible to nucleophilic attack.

(b) (i) $CH_3CH_2COCl + 2C_2H_5NH_2 \longrightarrow CH_3CH_2CONHC_2H_5 + C_2H_5NH_3{}^+Cl^-$ ✓ ✓

9

question

This equation is more difficult than that involving the alcohol because the amine reacts with the liberated hydrogen chloride to produce a salt. The following equation would score 1 mark:

$$CH_3CH_2COCl + C_2H_5NH_2 \longrightarrow CH_3CH_2CONHC_2H_5 + HCl$$

(ii)

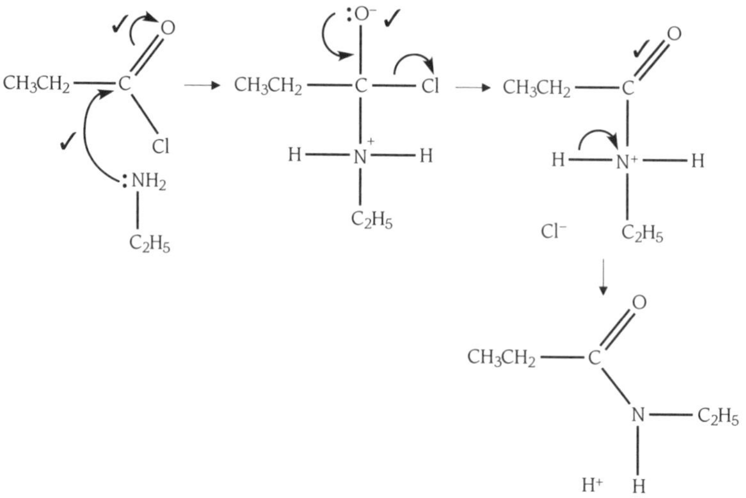

The mechanism is similar to the reaction of acyl chloride with an alcohol. The only difference is that the $-NH_2$ group replaces the $-OH$ group.

(iii) X:

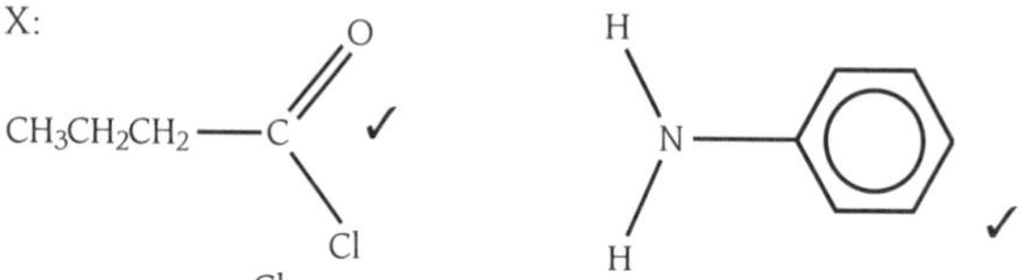

Y:

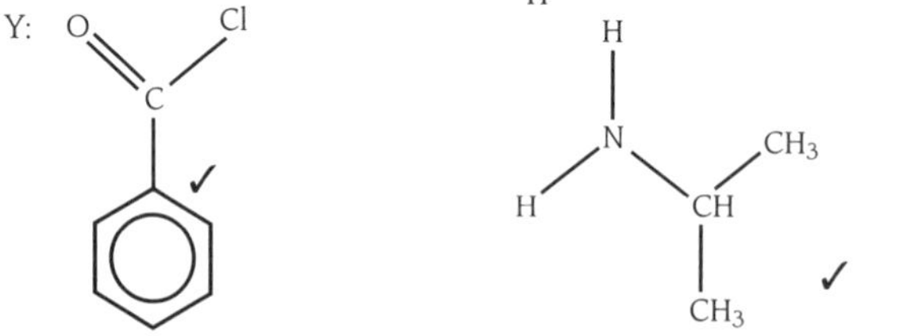

To predict the acyl chlorides and amines used, split the amide at the C–N bond and add Cl to the carbon of the C=O group and H to the N of the NH group.

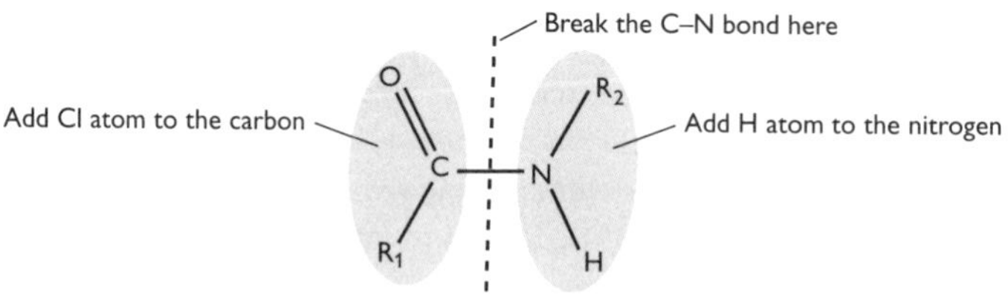

Break the C–N bond here

Add Cl atom to the carbon

Add H atom to the nitrogen

(c) (i)

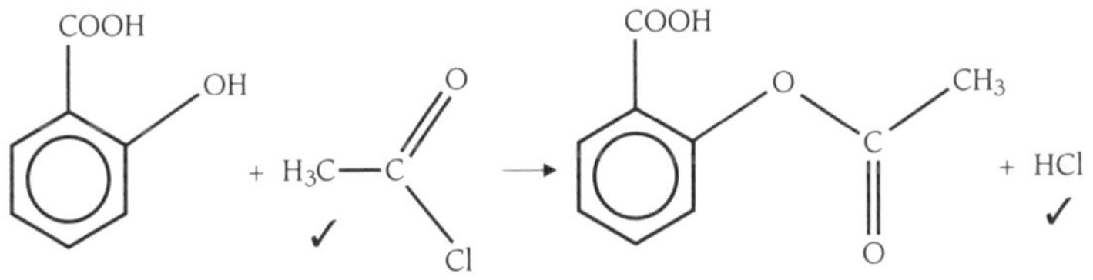

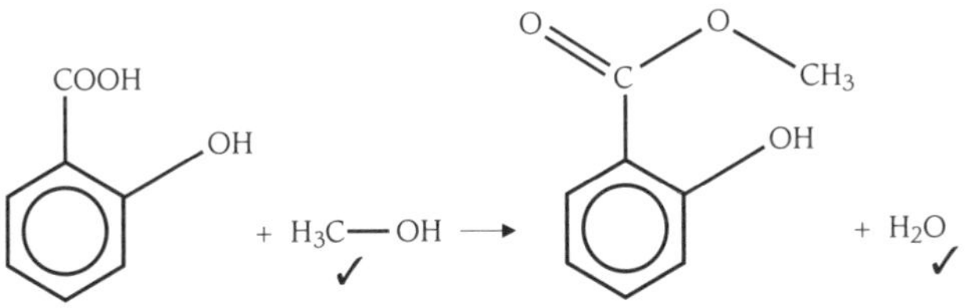

2-hydroxybenzenecarboxylic acid possesses both an –OH group and a –COOH group. The –OH group reacts with an acyl chloride (CH_3COCl) to produce an ester. The –COOH group reacts with the alcohol (CH_3OH) to produce a different ester. A common mistake is to omit the HCl or H_2O from the equation.

(ii) Concentrated sulphuric acid ✓

Carboxylic acids are less reactive than acyl chlorides. Esterification requires a catalyst, unlike acylation.

(iii) Ethanoic anhydride ✓

An alternative reagent to CH_3COCl is ethanoic anhydride and the equation is:

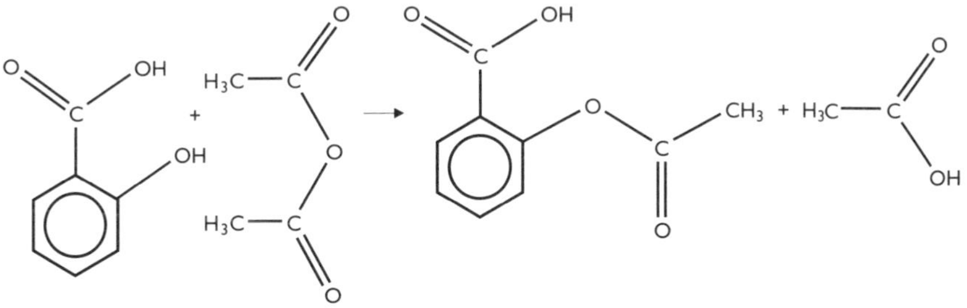

Ethanoic anhydride is the common reagent used in industry. If you have used this compound in part (i) then the alternative reagent in this section must be CH_3COCl.

(d) (i) C ✓, B ✓, B ✓

All these compounds will react with NaOH but only compound C will undergo hydrolysis to produce $C_6H_5COO^-Na^+$ and CH_3OH. Compound B will undergo nucleophilic addition–elimination reactions with ammonia to produce $C_6H_5CONH_2$ and NH_4Cl. Compound B is an acyl chloride, so it reacts with cold water in a nucleophilic addition–elimination reaction to produce C_6H_5COOH and HCl.

(ii)

COOH · · · CH₂—OH ✓ · · · (ester) + H₂O

(acyl chloride) + 2 (NH₂ ✓) → (amide) + NH₃⁺Cl⁻ ✓

Compound D is an ester, so compound A must react with an alcohol. To predict the alcohol needed, split the ester at the C–O bond and add a hydrogen atom to the $OCH_2C_6H_5$ part so that it becomes $HOCH_2C_6H_5$ (phenylmethanol, $C_6H_5CH_2OH$). Remember to include water in the final balanced equation. Compound E is an amide, so compound B must react with an amine. To predict the amine needed, split the amide at the C–N bond and add a hydrogen atom to the NHC_6H_5 part so that it becomes $NH_2C_6H_5$ (phenylamine, $C_6H_5NH_2$). The equation for this conversion is more difficult because the liberated HCl reacts with the phenylamine to produce the salt phenylammonium chloride, $C_6H_5NH_3^+Cl^-$.

Aromatic chemistry

(a) The structure of 4-phenylbut-1-ene is shown below:

Draw a diagram of the compound above and label on the diagram a
carbon–carbon bond that has a length of:
(i) 154 nm
(ii) 139 nm
(iii) 133 nm   (3 marks)

(b) The enthalpy of hydrogenation of compound X is $\Delta H = -120\,kJ\,mol^{-1}$.

Compound X

(i) Use this value to predict the enthalpy of hydrogenation of
compounds A to D below.   (4 marks)

Compound A

Compound B

Compound C

Compound D

In compounds C and D it is assumed that there are alternate carbon–carbon
single bonds and carbon–carbon double bonds in the cyclic part of the
molecule.
(ii) Explain why the enthalpy of hydrogenation of 4-phenylbut-1-ene is
approximately $-328\,kJ\,mol^{-1}$.   (2 marks)

(c) The structure of compound Y is shown below. It is formed in the nitration of 4-phenylbut-1-ene.

$$CH_2-CH_2-CH=C\begin{smallmatrix}H\\\\H\end{smallmatrix}$$

Compound Y

O_2N

(i) State the reagents needed for nitration. (2 marks)

(ii) Write an equation for the formation of compound Y from 4-phenylbut-1-ene. (1 mark)

(iii) Write a series of equations to show the formation of the nitronium ion (nitryl cation) during the nitration process. (3 marks)

(iv) Outline the mechanism for the nitration of 4-phenylbut-1-ene. (4 marks)

(v) Draw the structure of another possible product in the mononitration of 4-phenylbut-1-ene. (1 mark)

(d) Benzene can be converted into polystyrene in a three-stage process.

CH_2-CH_3　　　　　$CH=CH_2$

Step 1 → 　　Step 2 → 　　Step 3 → 　Polystyrene
or
poly(phenylethene)

(i) State the reagents required in step 1. (2 marks)

(ii) Write an equation for the formation of the electrophile in step 1. (1 mark)

(iii) Outline the mechanism for the reaction in step 1. (3 marks)

(iv) Write an equation for step 2. (1 mark)

(v) Write an equation for step 3. (2 marks)

(vi) In the conversion of benzene to propylbenzene, the propyl group undergoes rearrangement to produce a branched alkyl group in the final product, (1-methylethyl)benzene (cumene). This problem can be overcome by using acylation followed by reduction. Give the structure of the reagent used in acylation to produce propylbenzene. (1 mark)

Total: 30 marks

■ ■ ■

Grade-A answer to Question 10

(a)

(i) 154 nm ✓　　(iii) 133 nm ✓

(ii) 139 nm ✓

🖉 The principle being tested is that a carbon–carbon bond in benzene is intermediate in length between a shorter carbon–carbon double bond in an alkene and a longer carbon–carbon bond in an alkane. The 139 nm bond could be any of the six carbon–carbon bonds in benzene. The 154 nm bond could be either of the carbon–carbon single bonds. The 133 nm bond can only be the carbon–carbon double bond.

(b) (i) Compound A = $-240\,kJ\,mol^{-1}$ ✓; Compound B = $-240\,kJ\,mol^{-1}$ ✓; Compound C = $-360\,kJ\,mol^{-1}$ ✓; Compound D = $-480\,kJ\,mol^{-1}$ ✓

🖉 One C=C bond liberates $-120\,kJ\,mol^{-1}$ upon hydrogenation. Two C=C bonds would be expected to liberate $-240\,kJ\,mol^{-1}$, three C=C bonds would liberate $-360\,kJ\,mol^{-1}$ and four C=C bonds would liberate $-480\,kJ\,mol^{-1}$. This assumes there is no delocalisation of electrons in the structures.

(ii) The 4-phenylbut-1-ene should have an enthalpy of hydrogenation of $-480\,kJ\,mol^{-1}$ but it is $152\,kJ\,mol^{-1}$ more stable than expected ✓. This is because the alternate single and double bonds in the benzene ring exist as a ring of delocalised electrons, which causes this extra stability ✓.

🖉 In 4-phenylbut-1-ene there are four double bonds, three of which are in the benzene. However, the electrons in the benzene form a ring, or cloud, of delocalised electrons. This makes the compound more stable than expected, so the enthalpy of hydrogenation liberates less energy than anticipated, that is, $480 - 328 = 152\,kJ\,mol^{-1}$. This difference is called the delocalisation energy.

(c) (i) Concentrated nitric acid ✓ and concentrated sulphuric acid ✓

🖉 You must include the term 'concentrated' for both reagents.

(ii)

🖉 H_2SO_4 is not included in the final equation. A common mistake is to omit the H_2O.

(iii) $HNO_3 + H_2SO_4 \longrightarrow H_2NO_3^+ + HSO_4^-$ ✓
$H_2NO_3^+ \longrightarrow H_2O + NO_2^+$ ✓
$H_2SO_4 + H_2O \longrightarrow HSO_4^- + H_3O^+$ ✓

🖉 The H_2SO_4 acts as a strong acid and protonates the HNO_3, which decomposes readily to produce the NO_2^+ electrophile. The overall equation is:
$2H_2SO_4 + HNO_3 \longrightarrow NO_2^+ + H_3O^+ + 2HSO_4^-$

(iv)

C₄H₇ ... C₄H₇ ... C₄H₇ + H⁺

H — ... NO₂

NO₂

NO₂⁺

There are 4 marks for the mechanism. The first mark is for the curly arrow from the ring of delocalised electrons to the NO_2^+ ion, the second mark is for the structure of the intermediate, which must show the $-NO_2$ at the 4 position and the broken ring of electrons in the correct position. The third mark is for the curly arrow showing the hydrogen leaving and the electron pair from the bond returning to re-form the complete ring of delocalised electrons. The final mark is for the product, with a complete ring of delocalised electrons, and the H^+.

(v)

$CH_2—CH_2—CH=CH_2$

NO_2

An alternative is to show the $-NO_2$ group at the 3 position.

(d) (i) CH_3CH_2Cl ✓ and $AlCl_3$ ✓

Alternative reagents include other haloalkanes (e.g. CH_3CH_2Br) and other Lewis acid catalysts (e.g. $AlBr_3$ or $FeBr_3$).

(ii) $CH_3CH_2Cl + AlCl_3 \longrightarrow CH_3CH_2^+ + AlCl_4^-$ ✓

The $AlCl_3$ acts as a Lewis acid catalyst and accepts a lone pair to form $AlCl_4^-$.

(iii)

$CH_2^+—CH_3$ ... H, $CH_2—CH_3$ ... $CH_2—CH_3$ + H⁺

The mechanism follows the same principle as the nitration in part (c) (iv) with 1 mark for each curly arrow and 1 mark for the intermediate structure. It is essential that you are accurate when drawing the broken ring of delocalised electrons.

(iv) $CH_2—CH_3$ ... $CH=CH_2$ ... + H_2 ✓

📝 This is dehydrogenation. It requires a Fe_2O_3 catalyst at 600°C.

(v)

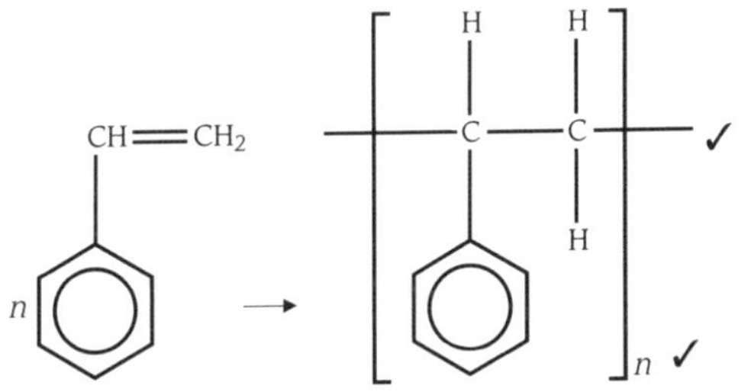

📝 In the polymerisation equation it is essential that the symbol 'n' is included before the monomer and after the repeating unit to gain the first mark. The second mark is for the structure of the polymer.

(vi)

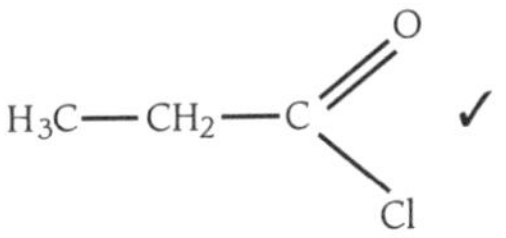

📝 An acyl chloride with three carbon atoms is required. CH_3CH_2COCl will produce the electrophile $CH_3CH_2CO^+$, which reacts in a similar way to the haloalkane to produce $C_6H_5COCH_2CH_3$. This compound is readily reduced to produce $C_6H_5CH_2CH_2CH_3$ and avoids the problem of rearrangement, which would give $C_6H_5CH(CH_3)_2$.

Question 11

Amines

(a) Write an equation for the reaction of propylamine with (i) water and
(ii) hydrochloric acid. Explain why propylamine is acting as a base in these
reactions. (3 marks)

(b) Explain why propylamine is a stronger base than ammonia. (2 marks)

(c) Consider the reaction schemes below, which summarise the two methods
available for the preparation of propylamine.

Method A

$$H_3C-CH_2-Br \xrightarrow{\text{Step 1}} H_3C-CH_2-CN \xrightarrow{\text{Step 2}} H_3C-CH_2-CH_2-NH_2$$

Method B

$$H_3C-CH_2-CH_2-Br \xrightarrow{\text{One step}} H_3C-CH_2-CH_2-NH_2$$

(i) Classify the reaction type in:
- method A, step 1
- method A, step 2
- method B (3 marks)

(ii) Write an equation for:
- method A, step 1
- method A, step 2
- method B (3 marks)

(iii) What is the main advantage of step 2 in method A over the single-step
method B in the preparation of propylamine? (2 marks)

(iv) Draw the mechanism for the formation of propylamine in method B. (4 marks)

(v) Give the structures of three other possible nitrogen-containing products
when propylamine is prepared from 1-bromopropane in method B. (3 marks)

(d) The pain-killing drug paracetamol is produced from phenol in the reaction
sequence outlined below.

OH   OH   OH   OH

Phenol $\xrightarrow{\text{Step 1}}$ NO_2 (A) $\xrightarrow{\text{Step 2}}$ NH_2 (B) $\xrightarrow{\text{Step 3}}$ $HN-\overset{\overset{\displaystyle O}{\|}}{C}-CH_3$ Paracetamol

(i) Explain why compound B is less basic than ammonia. (2 marks)

(ii) Classify the reaction type for each of the steps 1, 2 and 3. (3 marks)

(iii) Write an equation to describe each of the steps 1, 2 and 3. (3 marks)

(iv) State the reagents needed in step 2. (1 mark)

(v) State the role of compound B in step 3. (1 mark)

Total: 30 marks

Grade-A answer to Question 11

(a) (i) $CH_3CH_2CH_2NH_2 + H_2O \rightleftharpoons CH_3CH_2CH_2NH_3^+ + OH^-$ ✓
(ii) $CH_3CH_2CH_2NH_2 + HCl \longrightarrow CH_3CH_2CH_2NH_3^+ + Cl^-$ ✓
The propylamine donates an electron pair ✓, so is acting as a Lewis base.

An alternative answer for the third mark is that propylamine accepts a proton (or H^+ ion) and so is acting as a Brønsted–Lowry base.

(b) The alkyl group $(CH_3CH_2CH_2)-$ is electron releasing ✓. This makes the lone pair on the nitrogen more readily available ✓.

Various expressions are used to describe the electron-releasing effect of the alkyl group. The alkyl group 'has a positive inductive effect' or 'pushes electrons towards the nitrogen' are acceptable answers for the first mark.

(c) (i) Method A, step 1 is nucleophilic substitution ✓.
Method A, step 2 is reduction ✓.
Method B is nucleophilic substitution ✓.

Step 2 in method A could be classified as hydrogenation.

(ii) $CH_3CH_2Br + KCN \longrightarrow CH_3CH_2CN + KBr$ ✓
$CH_3CH_2CN + 2H_2 \longrightarrow CH_3CH_2CH_2NH_2$ ✓
$CH_3CH_2CH_2Br + 2NH_3 \longrightarrow CH_3CH_2CH_2NH_2 + NH_4Br$ ✓

In the first equation, NaCN could be used but not HCN. In the second, the symbol 4[H] could be used to represent the reducing agent. In the third, $2NH_3$ is essential because the liberated HBr reacts with the NH_3 to produce the salt NH_4Br.

(iii) In step 2 of method A there is only one product ✓ whereas in method B there is a risk of further substitution to produce a mixture of amines and the quaternary ammonium salt ✓.

The amines produced as a result of nucleophilic substitution still possess a lone pair. They can act as nucleophiles and attack the haloalkane, resulting in a mixture of products. The reaction stops when the quaternary ammonium salt is produced because the nitrogen has four groups attached and there is no lone pair available.

(iv)

There are 3 marks for the curly arrows and 1 mark for the intermediate structure. Common mistakes include omitting the lone pair from the nitrogen in ammonia, including a negative charge on the ammonia molecule and omitting the positive charge on the nitrogen in the intermediate structure.

(v) $(CH_3CH_2CH_2)_2NH$ ✓, $(CH_3CH_2CH_2)_3N$ ✓, $(CH_3CH_2CH_2)_4N^+Br^-$ ✓

💡 The amines continue to attack the original haloalkane to produce a mixture of secondary and tertiary amines. The final product is a quaternary ammonium salt.

(d) (i) The lone pair on the nitrogen atom in the $-NH_2$ is less available ✓ in compound B because it interacts with the delocalised electrons in the benzene ring ✓.

💡 Basicity is determined by the availability of the lone pair; this is stressed in the specification. Always approach it from this angle, rather than the ability to accept a proton.

(ii) Step 1 = nitration ✓, step 2 = reduction ✓, step 3 = acylation ✓

💡 The question asks for reaction *types* not names of mechanisms. However, acceptable answers would be, for step 1, 'electrophilic substitution' and, for step 3, 'nucleophilic addition–elimination'.

(iii)

HO—⬡ + HNO_3 ⟶ HO—⬡—NO_2 + H_2O ✓

HO—⬡—NO_2 + 6[H] ⟶ HO—⬡—NH_2 + $2H_2O$ ✓

HO—⬡—NH_2 + H_3C—C(=O)Cl ⟶ HO—⬡—NH—C(=O)—CH_3 + HCl ✓

💡 Concentrated sulphuric acid is used in nitration to generate NO_2^+ but is not included in the overall equation. A common mistake is to omit the H_2O. The alternative to 6[H] is $3H_2$ in the reduction of the NO_2 group. The alternative to ethanoyl chloride is ethanoic anhydride, which forms CH_3COOH rather than HCl.

(iv) Tin and concentrated hydrochloric acid ✓

💡 Alternative reagents in step 2 are hydrogen and a nickel catalyst.

(v) Compound B is acting as a nucleophile ✓.

💡 Step 3 is a nucleophilic addition–elimination reaction. The first step involves the attack by compound B on the electron-deficient carbon of the ethanoyl chloride. Compound B has a lone pair on the nitrogen of the $-NH_2$ group and donates it to the ethanoyl chloride, so it is acting as a nucleophile.

12

Amino acids

The structure of phenylalanine is shown below:

(a) Explain why phenylalanine exhibits optical isomerism, draw the structure of both enantiomers and explain how they could be distinguished from each other. (6 marks)

(b) Draw the structure of phenylalanine when it is in a solution of (i) sodium hydroxide and (ii) hydrochloric acid. (2 marks)

(c) Draw the structure of phenylalanine at its isoelectric point. (1 mark)

(d) Phenylalanine is isomeric with the compound benzocaine.

Benzocaine

State which compound has the higher melting point. Explain why. (3 marks)

(e) Draw the repeating unit when phenylalanine undergoes polymerisation. (1 mark)

(f) Draw the structure of the amino acid 2-aminopropanoic acid. Draw the structure of the dipeptide formed when phenylalanine reacts with 2-amino-propanoic acid and circle the peptide link in the dipeptide. (3 marks)

(g) Predict the structure of the organic product when phenylalanine reacts with ethanoyl chloride. (1 mark)

(h) Name, and outline the mechanism for, the reaction of phenylalanine with ethanoyl chloride. Use RNH_2 to represent the structure of phenylalanine. (5 marks)

(i) Consider the tripeptide shown below:

(i) Copy the structure of the tripeptide then label each chiral centre present in the tripeptide with an asterisk (*). Circle the peptide links.

12

(ii) State the type of intermolecular force that holds together molecules of the tripeptide.

(iii) Name a reagent that would hydrolyse the tripeptide. Draw the structure of the constituent amino acids that would result from the hydrolysis.

(8 marks)

Total: 30 marks

■ ■ ■

Grade-A answer to Question 12

(a) Phenylalanine is a chiral molecule because it contains an asymmetric carbon atom, that is, one of the carbon atoms has four different groups attached ✓.

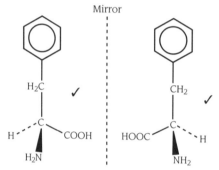

Each enantiomer will rotate ✓ plane-polarised light ✓ equally in opposite directions ✓.

The first mark is for including any expression that conveys the idea of chirality, for example: asymmetric carbon atom; chiral centre indicated on the molecule; carbon with four different groups attached. When drawing the enantiomers, it is essential that you emphasise the three-dimensional tetrahedral nature of the molecule and that the enantiomers are mirror images of each other. Finally, you must mention plane-polarised light or the use of a polarimeter, otherwise you lose the last 3 marks. Common mistakes include using the word 'reflect' rather than 'rotate' and stating that the light is rotated by different amounts rather than in opposite directions.

(b) (i) The structure in NaOH will be: **(ii)** The structure in HCl will be:

Amino acids are both basic (due to the $-NH_2$ group) and acidic (due to the $-COOH$ group). When predicting the reactions of amino acids, treat the two functional groups separately. Addition of an alkali leads to a reaction with the acid part of the molecule to produce a salt of the type $H_2NRCOO^-Na^+$. Addition of an acid leads to a reaction with the basic part of the molecule to produce a salt of the type $HOOCRNH_3^+Cl^-$.

(c) The structure at the isoelectric point will be the zwitterion.

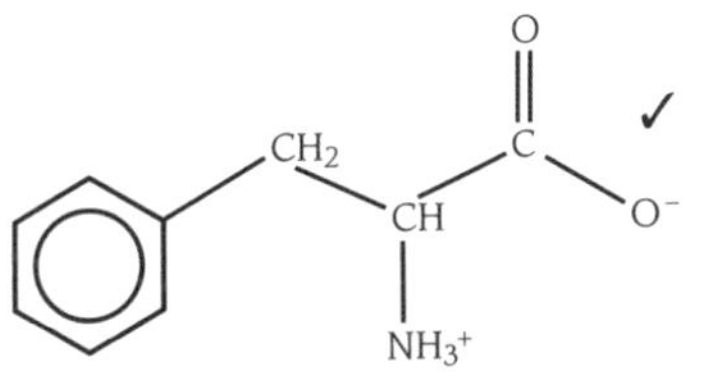

☑ At the isoelectric point, a zwitterion exists because the acid part of the molecule has donated an H^+ ion to the basic part of the molecule, to give COO^- and NH_3^+.

(d) Phenylalanine will have the higher melting point ✓ because it will exist as zwitterions ✓, with strong electrostatic forces of attraction between oppositely charged ions ✓. Benzocaine will have hydrogen bonding ✓.

☑ There are four marking points, of which three may be awarded. The first mark is for the correct initial statement. If this is incorrect, no further marks can be awarded.

(e)

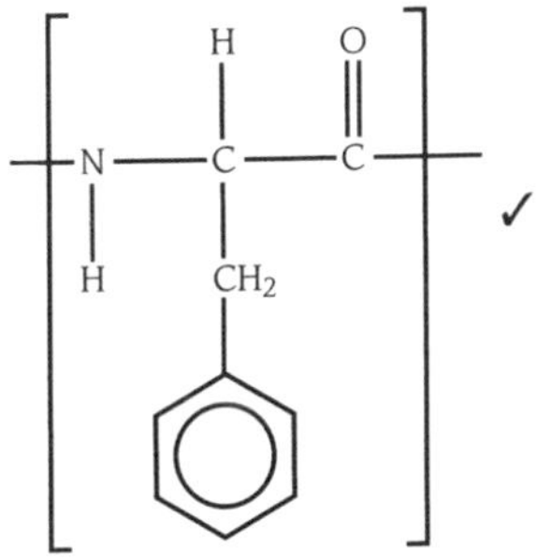

☑ When predicting the structure of the repeating unit when an amino acid polymerises, you must draw the structure so that the $-NH_2$ group is on one side of the molecule and the $-COOH$ is on the other side. Then remove an H from the $-NH_2$ group and the OH from the $-COOH$ group and replace them with lines that go through the brackets.

(f)

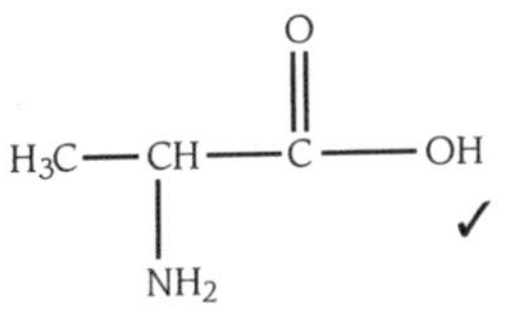

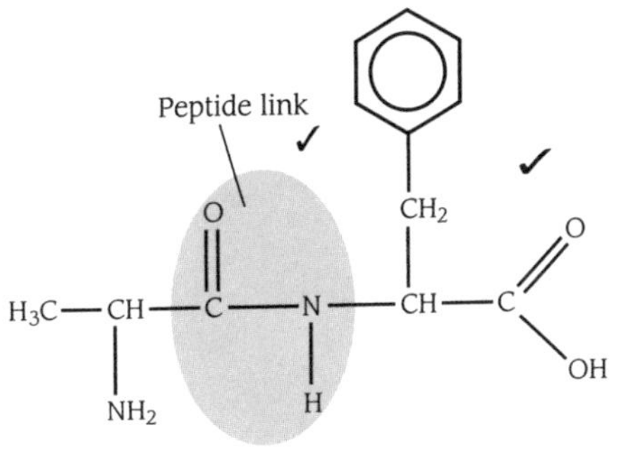

✓ An alternative structure is:

Peptide link ✓

(g)

✓ In this reaction, you are using your knowledge of amine chemistry to predict the product. The lone pair on the nitrogen of the –NH$_2$ group will attack the electron-deficient carbon atom of the ethanoyl chloride.

(h) Nucleophilic addition–elimination ✓

✓ This is a nucleophilic addition–elimination reaction, which leads to the formation of an amide. The rest of the amino acid molecule plays no part in the reaction, so it is given the symbol R. RNH$_2$ reacts in a similar way to any amine.

(i) (i)

✓ Peptide links

(ii) Hydrogen bonding ✓

(iii) Sodium hydroxide ✓; the constituent amino acids would be:

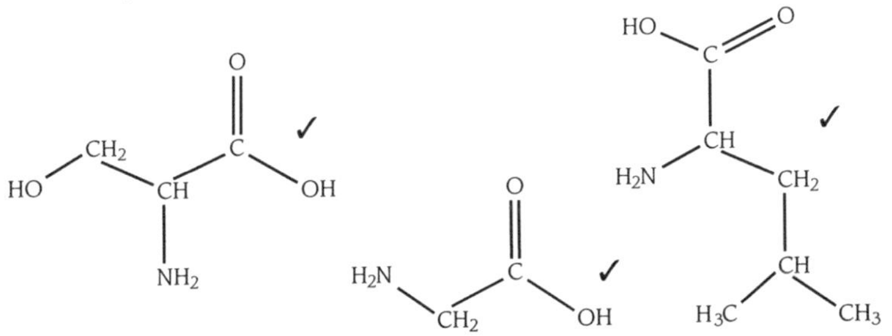

🔁 Looking for carbon atoms with four different groups attached identifies the chiral centres. There are 2 marks in part (i) for the two chiral centres. A peptide link is a –CONH– group and identifying both peptide links will gain the third mark. The inter-molecular forces are hydrogen bonds, owing to the presence of the –NH– and C=O groups. The peptide links are susceptible to acid (e.g. with HCl) or alkaline hydrolysis and will split at the C–N bond to regenerate the original amino acids. If alkaline hydrolysis is used, then the amino acids form salts of the type $H_2NRCOO^-Na^+$. If acid hydrolysis is used, then the amino acids form salts of the type $Cl^-H_3N^+RCOOH$, so alternatives to this grade-A answer are acceptable.

uestion 13

Polymers

(a) Draw the repeating units and name the addition polymers formed from the following monomers:

(i) propene

(ii) chloroethene (vinyl chloride)   (4 marks)

(b) Write equations for the formation of the following addition polymers:

(i) poly(propenenitrile)

(ii) poly(tetrafluoroethene) or PTFE   (4 marks)

(c) The monomer methyl 2-methylpropenoate (methyl methacrylate) undergoes addition polymerisation to produce a polymer used in the production of Perspex. Draw the repeating unit of this polymer and state the name of the polymer.

Methyl 2-methylpropenoate   (2 marks)

(d) Nylon-6,10 is formed from the monomers decanedioyl chloride and hexane-1,6-diamine.

(i) Draw the structures of decanedioyl chloride and hexane-1,6-diamine.

(ii) Show how these two compounds combine to form the polyamide nylon-6,10. Show clearly the repeating unit of nylon-6,10 and identify the small molecules lost in the formation of the polymer.   (4 marks)

(e) Draw the repeating units formed by the following amino acids:

(i) Glycine

(ii) Phenylalanine

(iii) Leucine

(3 marks)

(f) The following structure shows the compound caprolactam:

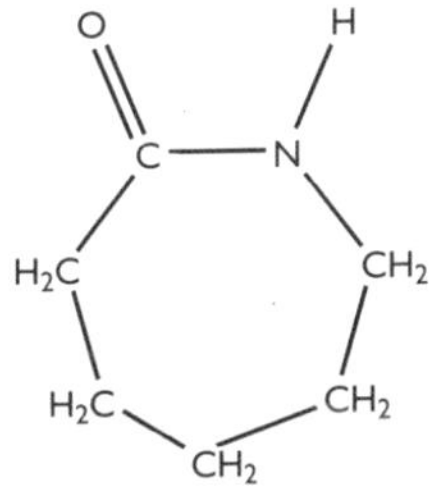

(i) When it is heated strongly, the caprolactam ring opens, which leads to the formation of a linear polyamide. Draw the repeating unit of this polyamide. (1 mark)

(ii) Explain why the linear polyamide formed can bind together to form strong fibres. (2 marks)

(g) Kevlar is an aromatic polyamide formed from the reaction of benzene-1,4-dicarboxylic acid and benzene-1,4-diamine. Kevlar has very high tensile strength and is used for lightweight bulletproof vests.

(i) Draw the structures of the two monomers used in this reaction. (2 marks)

(ii) Draw the structure of the repeating unit of Kevlar. (1 mark)

(h) Consider the following polymer chains labelled A to C:

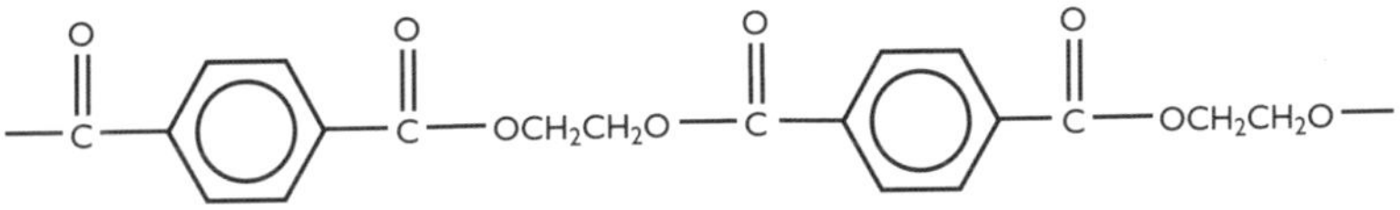

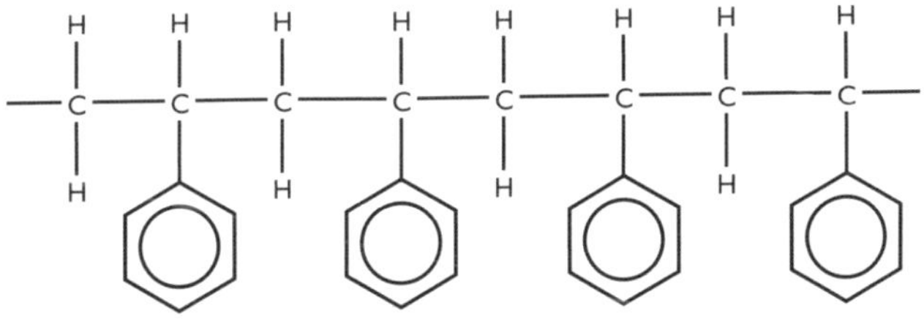

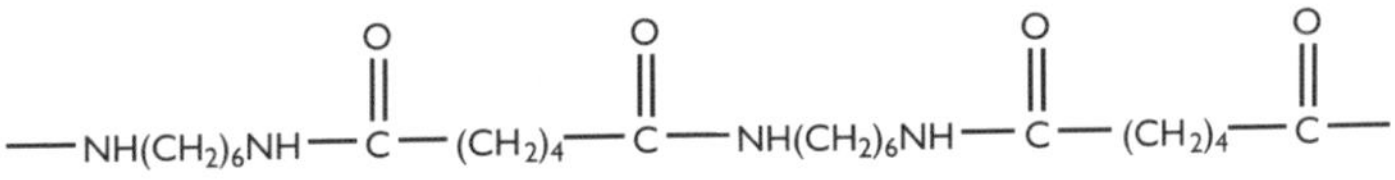

Using the letters A to C, identify the polymer(s):

(i) formed by addition polymerisation

(ii) formed by condensation polymerisation

(iii) held together by van der Waals forces only

(iv) held together by hydrogen bonding

(v) which are biodegradable (7 marks)

Total: 30 marks

13

question

Grade-A answer to Question 13

(a) (i)

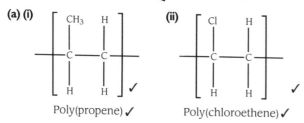

Poly(propene) ✓

(ii)

Poly(chloroethene) ✓

📝 Draw out the structures fully so that the positions of the methyl group in poly(propene) and of the chlorine atom in poly(chloroethene) are clear. A common mistake is to show poly(propene) as a three-carbon repeating unit with no branching, $-(CH_2CHCH_2)-$. When predicting the structure of an addition polymer, draw the C=C, draw the rest of the attached groups at right angles to this double bond, then open up the double bond to produce the bonds going through the brackets to make the repeating unit. Do not forget to add the 'n'. This is shown below for the poly-merisation of propene.

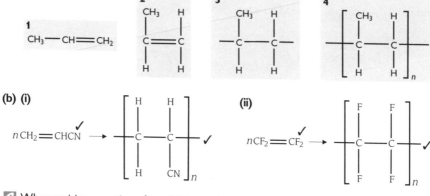

(b) (i)

$n\,CH_2{=}CHCN \longrightarrow$ ✓

(ii)

$n\,CF_2{=}CF_2 \longrightarrow$ ✓

📝 When writing equations for addition polymerisation reactions, you must include the monomer and the symbol 'n' in order to gain the first mark. The second mark is for the structure of the repeating unit.

(c)

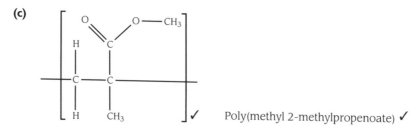

✓ Poly(methyl 2-methylpropenoate) ✓

📝 Do not be intimidated by the more complex monomer and its name. If you follow the four stages above, you will be able to predict the structure of any addition polymer.

To name an addition polymer, place the name of the monomer in brackets, then write 'poly' in front of the brackets.

(d) (i)

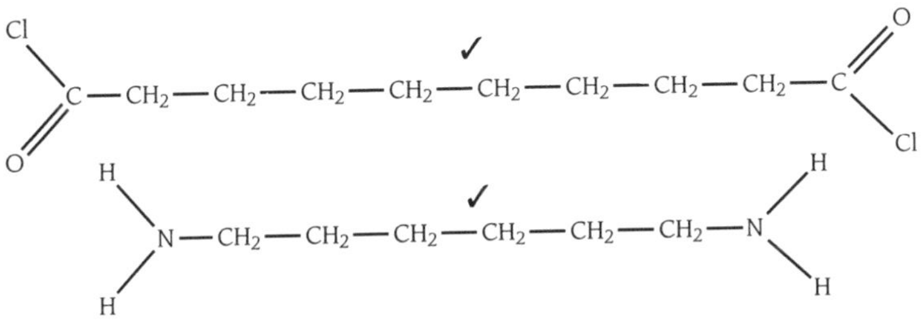

(ii)

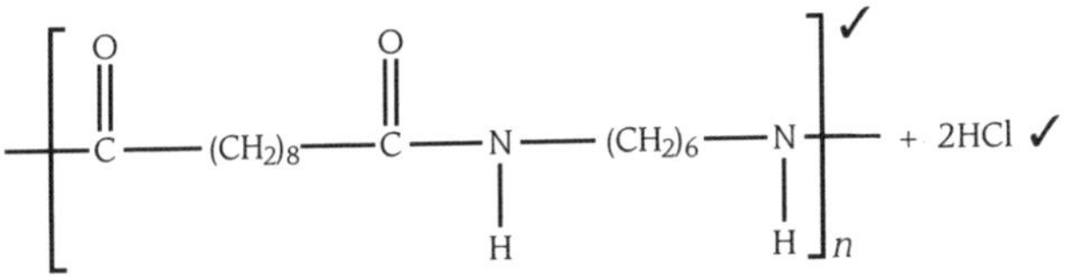

$$+ 2HCl ✓$$

💡 The most common mistake in this type of question is to include too many carbon atoms in the decanedioyl chloride. Remember that the –COCl groups at each end of the molecule provide two of the carbons, so only eight CH_2 groups are required. When drawing the repeating unit of the condensation polymer, it is important that the covalent bonds go through the brackets. If you have drawn the polyamide correctly, there will be a C=O group at one end and an NH group at the other.

(e)

(i)

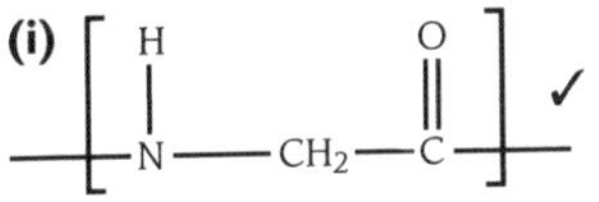

(ii)

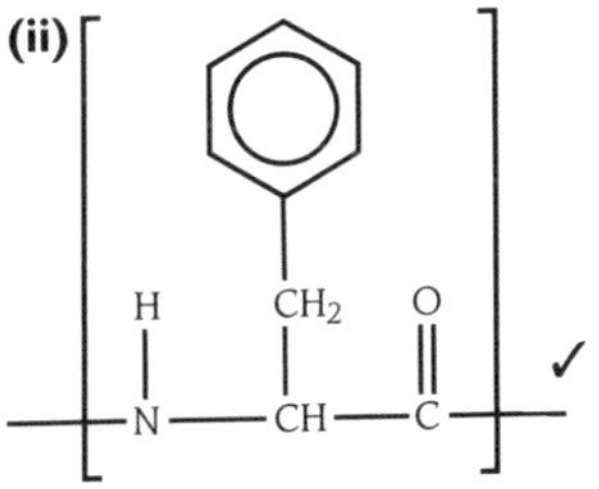

(iii)

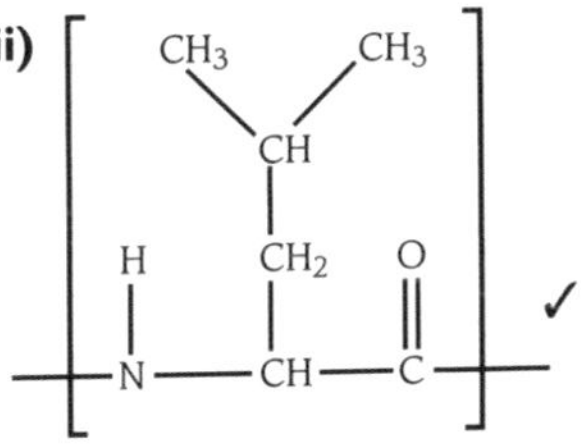

💡 Amino acids undergo self-polymerisation. Always draw the molecule with the $-NH_2$ group at one end and the –COOH at the other. To convert it into the polymer, take H from the $-NH_2$ and OH from the –COOH. This is shown for alanine below.

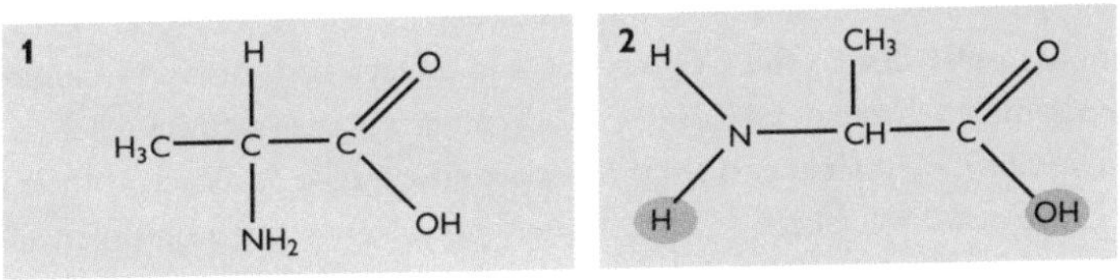

13

question

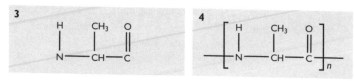

(f) (i)

$$\left[\begin{array}{c} H \\ | \\ N \end{array} - (CH_2)_5 - \begin{array}{c} O \\ || \\ C \end{array} \right]$$ ✓

(ii) The fibres will be held together by strong intermolecular forces ✓ due to hydrogen bonding ✓.

🖉 When this cyclic amide splits, the C–N bond of the peptide link breaks. The repeating unit can then be predicted using the four stages shown above. This is a polyamide and the presence of the NH and the C=O groups in the peptide links leads to the formation of hydrogen bonds between the polyamide chains.

(g) (i)

(structure) ✓   (structure) ✓

(ii)

(structure) ✓

🖉 The structures of the monomers are relatively easy to predict from their names. In this reaction, the OH is lost from the –COOH groups and the H is lost from the –NH$_2$ group to produce the polymer and molecules of water. This polyamide is formed by condensation polymerisation.

(h) (i) B ✓
(ii) A ✓ and C ✓
(iii) B ✓
(iv) C ✓
(v) A ✓ and C ✓

🖉 Addition polymerisation leads to the formation of polyalkenes, whereas condensation polymerisation leads to the formation of polyesters or polyamides. Polyalkenes are non-polar hydrocarbon chains which attract each other by van der Waals forces. Polyesters are polar due to the COO group and attract each other by dipole–dipole forces. Polyamides contain NH and C=O groups so they attract each other by hydrogen bonding. Polyesters and polyamides are susceptible to attack at their linkages so they can be easily broken down, whereas polyalkenes are non-polar, inert and non-biodegradable.

(iii)

and

5   **6**

(iv)

and

7   **8**

(16 marks)

Total: 30 marks

■ ■ ■

Grade-A answer to Question 15

(a) (i) Step 1 = electrophilic substitution ✓; step 3 = nucleophilic substitution ✓

🗨 The question asks you state the type of mechanism and not the type of reaction, so 'nitration' for step 1 and 'hydrolysis' for step 3 would not be accepted.

(ii) Step 4 = oxidation ✓; step 5 = esterification ✓; step 6 = reduction ✓

🗨 This question asks for the reaction types and there are no alternative answers for steps 4 and 5. However, in step 6, 'hydrogenation' would be acceptable.

(iii) Step 2: $CH_3-C_6H_4-NO_2 + Cl_2 \longrightarrow ClCH_2-C_6H_4-NO_2 + HCl$ ✓✓
Step 4: $HOCH_2-C_6H_4-NO_2 + 2[O] \longrightarrow HOOC-C_6H_4-NO_2 + H_2O$ ✓✓
Step 6: $CH_3CH_2OOC-C_6H_4-NO_2 + 6[H] \longrightarrow CH_3CH_2OOC-C_6H_4-NH_2 + 2H_2O$ ✓✓

🗨 In each of these equations, the benzene ring can either be represented by a hexagon with a ring of delocalised electrons inside or by $-C_6H_4-$ (not C_6H_6 because two of the hydrogen atoms have been replaced by other substituents). In steps 4 and 6, the oxidising agents and reducing agents are represented by [O] and [H]. An alternative to 6[H] in the last equation would be $3H_2$.

(iv) Dilute sulphuric acid ✓ and potassium dichromate(VI) ✓ under reflux ✓

🗨 Acidified potassium dichromate(VI) would score the first 2 marks. Reflux conditions ensure that the primary alcohol is completely oxidised to the carboxylic acid.

(b) (i) Add Tollens' reagent ✓: compound 1 — no reaction ✓; compound 2 — produces a silver mirror ✓

15
question

✏ This question is asking you to distinguish between an aldehyde and a ketone, so there are alternative answers. The equation remains the same but the requirements for the first 3 marks are different. Alternative 1: add Fehling's solution and heat — the ketone will give no reaction but the aldehyde will produce a red precipitate. Alternative 2: add acidified potassium dichromate(VI) — the ketone will give no reaction but the aldehyde will change the colour of the solution from orange to green. Alternative 3: add acidified potassium manganate(VII) — the ketone will give no reaction but the aldehyde will decolorise the purple solution.

(ii) Add acidified potassium dichromate(VI) and warm ✓: compound 3 — no reaction ✓; compound 4 — colour changes from orange to green ✓

$$H_3C-\overset{\overset{\displaystyle CH_3}{|}}{\underset{\underset{\displaystyle H}{|}}{C}}-CH_2-OH + 2[O] \longrightarrow H_3C-\overset{\overset{\displaystyle CH_3}{|}}{\underset{\underset{\displaystyle H}{|}}{C}}-\overset{\overset{\displaystyle O}{\diagup}}{\underset{\underset{\displaystyle OH}{\diagdown}}{C}} + H_2O ✓$$

✏ This pair of compounds comprises a tertiary alcohol and a primary alcohol, so the use of acidified potassium dichromate(VI) is the obvious test. An alternative would be to add acidified potassium manganate(VII) — the tertiary alcohol will give no reaction but the primary alcohol will decolorise the purple solution.

(iii) Add bromine water ✓: compound 5 — no reaction ✓; compound 6 — decolorises the bromine ✓

$$\text{(diagram)} + 2Br_2 \longrightarrow \text{(diagram)} ✓$$

✏ This pair of compounds comprises an alkane and an alkene, so the use of bromine water or bromine is the obvious choice. You must show the alkene reacting with 2 moles of bromine in the equation. An alternative answer would be to add an alkaline solution of potassium manganate(VII), which would give no reaction with the alkane but would produce a brown precipitate with the alkene. Hydrogen in the presence of a nickel catalyst is not acceptable as a simple chemical test.

(iv) Add sodium hydrogencarbonate ✓: compound 7 — liberates carbon dioxide ✓; compound 8 — no reaction ✓

$$\text{(diagram)} + NaHCO_3 \longrightarrow \text{(diagram)} + H_2O + CO_2 ✓$$

The final pair of compounds comprises a carboxylic acid and an ester, so the addition of any metal carbonate or metal hydrogencarbonate to produce carbon dioxide is acceptable. Other alternative answers include the addition of PCl_5, which would produce misty fumes of HCl with the acid but give no reaction with the ester. Addition of a suitable metal, such as magnesium, would produce hydrogen gas with the acid but give no reaction with the ester. Addition of a named indicator, such as litmus, which would turn red with the acid and show no change with the ester, is acceptable but it would be difficult to score the equation mark.

Question 16

Structure determination

You will need to use the data below in these questions.

Proton NMR chemical shift data

Type of proton	Chemical shift, δ/ppm
RCH_3	0.7–1.2
R_2CH_2	1.2–1.4
R_3CH	1.4–1.6
$RCOCH_3$	2.1–2.6
$ROCH_3$	3.1–3.9
$RCOOCH_3$	3.7–4.1
ROH	0.5–5.0

Infrared absorption data

Type of bond	Wavenumber/cm⁻¹
C–H	2850–3300
C–C	750–1100
C=C	1620–1680
C=O	1680–1750
C–O	1000–1300
O–H (alcohols)	3230–3550
O–H (acids)	2500–3000

An organic compound X has the following percentage composition by mass: 54.5% carbon, 9.1% hydrogen and 36.4% oxygen. It produces the following spectra:

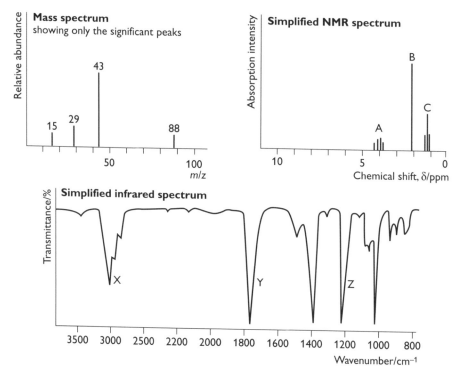

(a) (i) Deduce the empirical formula of compound X. (3 marks)

(ii) Use the mass spectrum to deduce the molecular formula of compound X. (2 marks)

(iii) Use the table of data to identify the bonds responsible for the absorptions at X, Y and Z in the infrared spectra. (3 marks)

(iv) Explain why the infrared spectrum confirms that compound **X** cannot be a
carboxylic acid. (2 marks)

(b) The simplified high-resolution NMR spectrum of compound **X** shows three
signals at **A**, **B** and **C**. The measured integration trace for these peaks gives a
ratio of 1.2:1.8:1.8 and the signals occur at chemical shift values of $\delta = 4.1$,
$\delta = 2.1$ and $\delta = 1.2$, respectively.

  (i) How many different types of proton are present in compound **X**? (1 mark)

  (ii) What is the actual whole number ratio of the numbers of each type of proton? (1 mark)

  (iii) Use the table of data to suggest the identity of the group that causes the
signal at $\delta = 2.1$. (1 mark)

  (iv) The peaks at $\delta = 4.1$ and $\delta = 1.1$ are caused by the presence of an alkyl group.
Identify the group and explain the splitting pattern. (3 marks)

(c) Write an equation to show the fragmentation of the molecular ion in the mass
spectrometer that leads to the formation of the most abundant peak in the
mass spectrum shown in part (a) above. (3 marks)

(d) Draw the structure of compound **X**. (1 mark)

(e) Low-resolution NMR spectroscopy can be used to distinguish between three
isomeric carbonyl compounds **A**, **B** and **C**, which gave molecular ions with a
mass:charge (m/z) ratio of 72 in their mass spectra. Compounds **A** and **B** both
have three peaks in their low-resolution NMR spectra with the ratio of peak
areas being 3:2:3 for compound **A** and 6:1:1 for compound **B**. In the low-resolution
NMR spectrum of compound **C** there are four peaks, with a ratio of 3:2:2:1.
Identify compounds **A**, **B** and **C**. (3 marks)

(f) Compound **D** is a saturated hydrocarbon, which also gives a molecular ion with
an m/z ratio of 72 in its mass spectrum. The low-resolution NMR spectrum of
compound **D** shows only one peak. Deduce the molecular formula of compound **D**
and draw its structure. (2 marks)

(g) Alcohols and ethers have the same general formula, $C_nH_{2n+2}O$. Ethers contain the
C–O–C linkage, for example, as in methoxyethane, $H_3C-O-CH_2CH_3$. Each of the
alcohols or ethers described below has the molecular formula $C_4H_{10}O$.

Compound	Type of compound	Number of peaks in low-resolution NMR	Ratio of peak area
E	Ether	4	3:2:2:3
F	Alcohol	2	9:1
G	Ether	2	3:2

  (i) Use this information to identify compounds **E**, **F** and **G**. (3 marks)

  (ii) Ethers and alcohols can be distinguished by studying their infrared spectra.
Using the table of data at the start of this section, state where, other than
the fingerprint region, their infrared spectra will be different. Explain what
causes the difference. (2 marks)

Total: 30 marks

16

question

Grade-A answer to Question 16

(a) (i) Atoms: $\qquad$ carbon $= \dfrac{54.5}{12}$ $\qquad$ hydrogen $= \dfrac{9.1}{1}$ $\qquad$ oxygen $= \dfrac{36.4}{16}$ ✓

Moles: $\qquad\qquad$ $= 4.54$ $\qquad\qquad$ $= 9.1$ $\qquad\qquad$ $= 2.275$ ✓

Simplest ratio: $\qquad$ $= 2$ $\qquad\qquad$ $= 4$ $\qquad\qquad$ $= 1$

Empirical formula $\quad = C_2H_4O$ ✓

☑ The correct answer scores 3 marks. However, it is essential that you show your working because there are always marks available for each stage of the calculation. If you make a careless mistake then consequential marks can be awarded.

(ii) The largest m/z value occurs at 88 ✓. This is twice the value of the empirical molecular mass, so the molecular formula must be $C_4H_8O_2$ ✓.

☑ The peak with the largest m/z value is produced by the molecular ion and gives the relative molecular mass of the compound. The molecular formula must be a whole number multiple of the empirical formula.

(iii) Absorption at X (3000 cm⁻¹) is due to the C–H bond ✓.
Absorption at Y (1750 cm⁻¹) is due to the C=O bond ✓.
Absorption at Z (1250 cm⁻¹) is due to the C–O bond ✓.

☑ Questions of this type are relatively easy and quite common.

(iv) There is no wide absorption between 2500 and 3000 cm⁻¹ ✓, so no acidic O–H bond is present ✓.

☑ When answering this type of question, quote the wavenumber value from the table because this is always allocated a mark. A wide absorption is characteristic of an O–H group, but remember there are two types, O–H in alcohols and O–H in acids, so you must specify which one is causing the absorption.

(b) (i) There are three different types of proton present ✓.

☑ The number of signals in an NMR spectrum indicates the number of different types or non-equivalent protons present in the compound. In this case, three signals means three different types of proton.

(ii) The ratio is 2:3:3 ✓.

☑ The ratio of 1.2:1.8:1.8 simplifies to 1:1.5:1.5 so the simplest whole number ratio of the protons must be 2:3:3.

(iii) The group causing the signal at $\delta = 2.1$ is $RCOCH_3$ ✓.

☑ This is found from the chemical shift values in the table of data. It has a relative intensity of 3 because there are three protons in a methyl group.

(iv) An ethyl group, $CH_3CH_2–$, causes these signals ✓. The peak at $\delta = 4.1$ is due to the CH_2 protons. It is split into a quartet because there are three equivalent adjacent protons (the CH_3 group) ✓. The peak at $\delta = 1.1$ is due to the CH_3

protons. It is split into a triplet because there are two equivalent adjacent protons (the CH_2 group) ✓.

☑ The peak at δ = 4.1 has a relative intensity of 2 because there are two protons in a CH_2 group. The splitting pattern is predicted using the $n + 1$ rule, that is, it has three adjacent protons, so this splits the peak into four (a quartet). The peak at δ = 1.1 has a relative intensity of 3 because there are three protons in a CH_3 group. Again, using the $n + 1$ rule, it is split into a triplet by the two adjacent protons in the CH_2 group.

(c) $[C_4H_8O_2]^{+\bullet}$ ✓ $\longrightarrow$ CH_3CO^+ ✓ + $C_2H_5O^{\bullet}$ ✓

☑ When writing the equation for the fragmentation of the molecular ion, you must include the 'plus' and the 'dot' to show the radical cation splitting into the cation (which is detected and produces a signal) and the radical (which is not detected).

(d) Ratio 3:2:3 protons from NMR

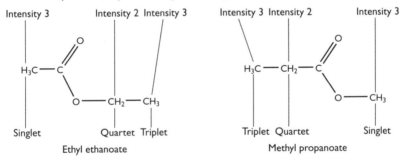

☑ There are two esters that would produce a ratio of 2:3:3 in their low-resolution spectra and a pattern of quartet, singlet and triplet. These are shown below.

Ethyl ethanoate   Methyl propanoate

The structure of ethyl ethanoate is correct because it matches the fragmentation pattern of the mass spectrum. If the compound had been methyl propanoate, it would have fragmented to produce the acylium ion $CH_3CH_2CO^+$ and $CH_3O^{\bullet}$, and the acylium ion would be detected at an m/z of 57 rather than at 43, which is caused by CH_3CO^+.

(e)

A $H_3C-C(O)-CH_2-CH_3$ ✓

B   CH₃ — $H_3C-C(CH_3)(H)-C(O)H$ ✓

C $H_3C-CH_2-CH_2-C(O)H$ ✓

☑ Carbonyl compounds have the general formula $C_nH_{2n}O$. A molecular mass of 72 indicates a molecular formula of C_4H_8O, that is, $(4 \times 12) + (8 \times 1) + (1 \times 16) = 72$.

There is only one ketone with the molecular formula C_4H_8O, which is butanone. Draw the aldehyde with the longest carbon chain to identify butanal; branching identifies the other aldehyde as methylpropanal. Once the compounds have been identified, they must be matched to the information provided by the low-resolution NMR spectra.

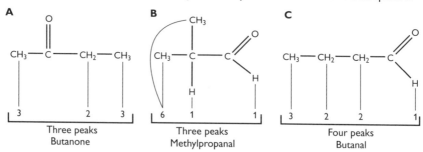

(f) The molecular formula is C_5H_{12} ✓. The structure of D is:

$$H_3C-\underset{\underset{CH_3}{|}}{\overset{\overset{CH_3}{|}}{C}}-CH_3 \checkmark$$

✏ The general formula of a non-cyclic saturated hydrocarbon is C_nH_{2n+2}. Since the M_r is 72, the molecular formula is C_5H_{12}, that is, $(5 \times 12) + (10 \times 1) + 2 = 72$. The compound must have four methyl groups because all the hydrogen atoms must be in the same environment.

(g) (i) E $H_3C-O-CH_2-CH_2-CH_3$ ✓   F $H_3C-\underset{\underset{CH_3}{|}}{\overset{\overset{OH}{|}}{C}}-CH_3$ ✓

   G $H_3C-CH_2-O-CH_2-CH_3$ ✓

✏ Compound E is methoxypropane. It must have four different types of proton because four peaks are produced. The molecule is unsymmetrical, so the CH_3 groups are in different environments and the CH_2 groups are also in different environments. Compound F is 2-methylpropan-2-ol. It has only two types of proton. The three methyl groups all contain equivalent protons, that is, they are in the same environment. The H in the OH group is the other type of proton present. Compound G is ethoxyethane. It is a symmetrical molecule. The two CH_3 groups contain protons in the same environment, as do the two CH_2 groups, which gives rise to a ratio of 6:4 or, more simply, 3:2.

(ii) The main difference will be an absorption at 3230–3550 cm⁻¹ ✓, due to the O–H bond in the alcohol F ✓, which will not be present in the ethers, E and G.

✏ When the question asks you to use the table of data, you *must* quote the absorption range in order to gain full marks. Here you must also specify that the absorption is caused by the alcohol O–H and not the acid O–H.